Cyberbullying and the Wild, Wild Web

Cyberbullying and the Wild, Wild Web

What Everyone Needs to Know

J. A. Hitchcock

ROWMAN & LITTLEFIELD
Lanham • Boulder • New York • London

Published by Rowman & Littlefield
A wholly owned subsidiary of The Rowman & Littlefield Publishing Group, Inc.
4501 Forbes Boulevard, Suite 200, Lanham, Maryland 20706
www.rowman.com

Unit A, Whitacre Mews, 26–34 Stannary Street, London SE11 4AB

British Library Cataloguing in Publication Information Available

Library of Congress Cataloging-in-Publication Data Available

978-1-4422-5117-5 (cloth)
978-1-4422-5118-2 (electronic)

♾ ™ The paper used in this publication meets the minimum requirements of American National Standard for Information Sciences—Permanence of Paper for Printed Library Materials, ANSI/NISO Z39.48–1992.

Printed in the United States of America

In memory of Phoebe,
the Cyber Crime Dog—the best dog ever.

Contents

Foreword

Every community has a netherworld: a neighborhood or area you simply avoid whenever possible, or, if you live there, hope someday to leave behind. The Internet has a netherworld as well, but you don't stumble into by happenstance; rather, usually it finds you.

If you do not know what I am talking about, take a moment to remember this day and your good fortune. When the netherworld does find you, the marvel that is the Internet suddenly looks different; now it has become your tormentor or your child's tormentor.

In this book, J. A. Hitchcock tackles the growing problem of cyberbullying. Amanda Todd, Megan Meier, Phoebe Prince, Tyler Clementi—all are names of teenagers we might have known years from now for the talents they possessed rather than for the cruelty that forced them to take their own lives.

Teens understand the danger of cyberbullying because almost half have been victimized in the past year, and two-thirds think it is a serious problem.[1] Yet, only one in six parents is aware of the scope or intensity of cyberbullying.[2]

The law and law enforcement have been slow to respond to online bullying and cyber harassment in general. Federal authorities only pursued ten of the 2.5 million cases of cyberstalking that occurred in the United States between 2010 and 2013.[3]

As Rep. Katherine Clark, a former prosecutor, has noted, a prevailing belief "says that if the problem's on the Internet, it's just not a real crime."[4]

Any victim of cybercrime will tell you that the harm we are talking about is anything but virtual.

As the founder of Working to Halt Online Abuse (WHO@), J. A. has stepped forward as a beacon of hope and a resource for victims for more than twenty years.

As a criminologist, she understood the value of data in measuring a problem, and WHO@'s annual reports provided some of the first warning signs of the growing problem of cyberstalking. J. A. also has been a tireless advocate for victims of cyber abuse, especially younger victims and their families, whom she helps through WHO@-KTD, WHO@'s kid and teen outreach arm.

As both an Internet lawyer who represents victims of cyber harassment and the host of an Internet radio show, I have worked with J. A. in helping victims respond to cyber harassment and highlighting the latest developments in cyber harassment. J. A. is an effective advocate for victims in part because she herself has been a victim of online abuse.

She already has written several books highlighting the dangers of this cyber netherworld, including *True Crime Online: Shocking Stories of Scamming, Stalking, Murder, and Mayhem*; and *Net Crimes & Misdemeanors: Outmaneuvering the Spammers, Swindlers, and Stalkers Who Are Targeting You Online*.

More important, J. A. has been a pioneer in reaching out to schools to educate children about how a student's supposedly innocuous social media posts and profiles can make her vulnerable to threats and harassment. With this book, J. A. makes a valuable contribution to helping parents and children alike understand the nature of the threat.

Some skeptics view bullying as a rite of passage and believe we need to encourage kids not to be so thin-skinned. All of us have dealt with bullies in our life. But we left them in the school yard; we did not take them home with us as kids do today with their mobile devices and social media on twenty-four hours a day, seven days a week. And the difference between being bullied in the school yard and being shamed across a platform viewable worldwide online is enormous.

Nobody would want their child to attempt to cross a busy highway unaccompanied, and the same is true for the information superhighway we call the Internet. A Japanese proverb says children grow up, with or without their parents. Our children will navigate through these dangers as best they can, but if we are going to prevent future bullycide deaths, parents will need to take the initiative to get a better understanding of what's going on. This book is an excellent resource for doing just that.

Past tragedies highlight cyberbullying as an important topic that needs to be addressed at the dinner table and in legislative committee rooms alike.

What exactly is cyberbullying, and what can be done in response?

Where is your child most at risk, and what do you do if your child is the cyberbully?

These are all questions that modern families must face. Luckily, J. A. addresses them in this book.

Although we mourn those we have lost along the way, we see signs of hope that maybe we are turning the corner on the prevailing view that somehow the Internet is the "Wild, Wild West."

Prosecution of and convictions for online harassment are increasing steadily. In a recent case, the Massachusetts attorney general declared, "We will not tolerate people hiding behind their computer screens and committing criminal intimidation or harassment."[5]

In the Tyler Clementi case, the roommate who set up the webcam streaming Clementi's intimate moments was prosecuted and convicted. To their credit, Clementi's family has established the Tyler Clementi Institute for CyberSafety, which runs an annual Internet Safety Conference at New York University Law School and the nation's first pro bono law school clinic representing victims of cyber harassment.

What the Clementis have shown is that we need to protect our children through vigilance, enforcement, and education. I congratulate J. A. for urging us forward with this important book, which not only highlights a growing problem, but also provides tools for families to protect their children.

As she has done for more than two decades, once again J. A. has provided clarity and hope in an area where so often they are lacking.

—Bennet Kelley

Bennet Kelley is the founder of the Internet Law Center (www.Internet lawcenter.net) in Santa Monica, California, and host of *Cyber Law and Business Report* on WebmasterRadio.fm. His practice includes representing victims of cyber harassment.

Bennet Kelley, Internet Law Center. © Bennet Kelley.

Introduction

When I was stalked online in 1996, I had no clue how much harassment, stalking, and bullying would happen over the coming years. At that time, I felt alone—no organizations existed to help online victims like me, no laws were in place to hold stalkers accountable, and law enforcement could do nothing for me.

To make a long story short, I was helping fellow writers get back money they paid to what they thought was a legitimate literary agent. This "agency" turned out to be a scam, so I reported it to the New York attorney general's office because it was located in New York State.

Because I blew the whistle on the scam, the "agency" retaliated by pretending to be me online, posting on newsgroups as me trying to rile up people, then escalating the posts to include my home phone number and address and inviting people to share their "phantasies" with me for my alleged next book. You can read the whole story at jahitchcock.com/cyber stalked. But rest assured, my cyberstalkers eventually were caught and punished.

The resulting chaos that ensued took me ten years to resolve. During that time, I changed my phone number three times to a private number (the "agency" kept finding my new number), helped get the first e-mail harassment law passed in Maryland (where I lived at the time), spoke to local computer groups, and was interviewed by media in Washington, D.C., and Maryland.

I helped the Maryland State Police Department's Computer Crime Division with some of its first cases, and that began my career training law enforcement. I've trained law enforcement at the local, state, and federal levels, and I have traveled to nearly all fifty states and as far afield as South Korea, England, and Canada to speak about my experience and expertise.

I also cofounded an all-volunteer organization, Working to Halt Online Abuse (WHO@ at haltabuse.org) in February of 1997 with another cyberstalking victim after friends introduced us. She left to pursue her legal degree in 1999, and I took over as president.

WHO@ helps online victims age eighteen and older anywhere in the world who are being stalked or harassed online with instructions on how to deal with their cyberstalkers and cyberbullies. Over the years, we have found that we can help victims resolve their situation more than 70 percent of the time without involving law enforcement or other legal measures.

More states began to pass online harassment and cyberstalking laws after Maryland's, many I spurred on by testifying in person or in writing. The state of Maine, where I now live, passed its first cyberstalking law, which I cowrote with a now-retired Kennebunk detective, in 2001. Now all fifty states and several countries have the same or similar laws which are part of the discussion in this book.

In 2005, WHO@ started getting requests for help from students and parents. Students were being bullied and harassed online and had no idea what to do about it. After discussing it with my board, we decided to add WHO@-KTD (Working to Halt Online Abuse-Kids/Teen Division) at haltabusektd .org to help kids and teens under the age of eighteen and to provide resources and other information for parents, educators, and concerned adults.

I also began speaking at middle and high schools in 2005 about cyberbullying, social media safety, online predators, and eventually sexting, swatting, and smartphone apps. It's amazing how quickly the younger generation can adapt to new technologies, sometimes leaving parents and other adults feeling, well, stupid. That's where WHO@-KTD comes in, trying to keep up with what's new online that kids and teens are using.

When I speak to parents, I try to bring them up to speed on the latest websites or apps that their kids and teens may be using online.

At one presentation, during questions after my talk, one mother asked, "Can you move in with us?" Although the question generated some hearty laughter, it also showed how desperate some parents are when it comes to their children, the Internet, and cell phones.

I hope now to educate and inform you about cyberbullying: what it is, who cyberbullies are, and how to handle a cyberbullying situation, whether it's your child, your student, or someone else you may know who needs help.

This book also may help *you* with an online situation you may be experiencing. The tools I will share with you can be applied to almost anything that happens to someone online.

One thing I want to make unequivocally clear—the Internet is not a bad place. All Internet users are not bad. It's similar to your offline or real life—it includes good people and bad people, good "neighborhoods" and bad ones. It is up to you to choose where you go and how you interact. If you know a website or app may be "iffy," don't go there or use it. Stick with what you know, or ask around for advice.

The Internet has so much good going for it. It is wonderful for research, whether for school, pleasure, or work. It has a lot of fun entertainment, from games to YouTube and other video websites, to sites where you can spend time with faraway family members or old friends you have reconnected with or even new friends you've just met online or offline. Recipes, product reviews, free samples, surveys for gift cards, news articles and videos—you name it, you can probably find it online. And let's not forget shopping!

So take a deep breath, let it go, and read this book with an open mind. You may learn something you didn't know about cyberbullying and cyberbullies. You can share that knowledge to try to make the Internet a safer place for anyone online anywhere in the world.

CHAPTER ONE

Who Are Cyberbullies?

Although the majority of cyberbullies are kids and teens eighteen and under, some adults have nothing better to do than torment a young boy or girl into doing unimaginable things, even suicide.

That is what happened to Amanda Todd, who lived in Port Coquitlam, British Columbia, Canada.

Born in 1996, Amanda was a typical teenager: giggly, fun, and trusting. She met someone on Facebook in 2010 who flattered her to no end. He was charming, had a good sense of humor, and, after a while, it seemed like a relationship to her. She was ecstatic and in love! When he asked her to go on her webcam and take off her shirt to show him her breasts, she did, not thinking twice about it.

She trusted him.

That was her big mistake. He wanted more videos and photos of her breasts, and of her naked. She refused. He threatened to spread the photo he had of her breasts online if she didn't. She still refused.

At four in the morning in December of 2010, local police contacted Amanda: the photo of her breasts had been posted online and quickly was going viral. She was shocked, upset, and scared. People she knew, and even those she did not know, began harassing and bullying her online and offline, making crude comments about her breasts and saying she was a whore, among other things.

Her family moved, hoping to relieve her depression and anxiety, but she turned to drugs and alcohol for relief. Those didn't help, and a year later she discovered that a profile had been created on Facebook, using the topless photo of her as its profile photo. If that wasn't enough, this person then began making friends with her classmates and friends.

The bullying became so bad that Amanda's parents moved her to a different school. But she had had enough and drank chlorine bleach, hoping that she would die and get it over with. She didn't die . . . that time.

Her parents moved again, hoping a new school and new location would be a new start for their very troubled daughter. She began cutting herself because the depression wouldn't go away. The same person who harassed her online opened a new profile on Facebook with the photo of her breasts, contacted her new classmates, and began the bullying and humiliation all over again.

Although she saw a therapist, she finally was hospitalized for severe depression. This only made the online bullying worse. Classmates branded her a psycho, and crazy, and she spiraled down again.

On October 10, 2012, Amanda posted a video on YouTube.[1] She silently flashed cards about what had happened to her online, including "He sent me a message. It said . . . if you don't put on a show for me I will send ur boobs. He knew my adress [sic], school, relatives, friends, family names."

And "I'm stuck . . . what's left of my life now . . . nothing stops. I have nobody. I need someone. ↶ my name is Amanda Todd."

Four hours after posting the video, she allegedly hung herself and died.

Online came a mix of outpourings of sympathy, yet some still bullied her, calling her a coward and that she deserved to die, among other things.

A police investigation ensued. In January 2014, Dutch police arrested thirty-five-year-old Aydin C. (privacy laws there allow arrested individuals to remain anonymous) who was charged with indecent assault, extortion, Internet luring, criminal harassment, and distribution of child pornography for alleged activities against Amanda Todd and, as it turns out, other male and female victims under the age of eighteen. His case is still pending.[2]

In a strange twist, the suspect penned a letter proclaiming his innocence, allowing his full name, Aydin Coban, to be made public. He handwrote the four-page letter, giving it to his lawyer to send to the media. In it, he proclaimed that the media and public had branded him a monster.

"They pretend to be the judge, the jury and the executioner while committing character assassination by orchestrating a hate campaign against an individual on a scale rarely seen," he wrote.

He even claimed the Dutch police "infected" his computer to make it look like the messages sent to Amanda were from him and that he was framed by the police.

"There is more, but I'll mention those in court. All I wanted to say for now is in this open letter," Coban concluded.

So, cyberbullies can be anyone of any age, race, or gender.

A WHO@-KTD survey[3] in 2008 found that 43 percent of students were cyberbullied by someone they knew who was their age or in the same grade; the others did not know who was bullying.

According to a 2009 Cox Communications survey[4] called Profile of a Cyberbully:

- More were girls (59 percent girls versus 41 percent boys).
- They spend more time online per week (38.4 hours, compared to 26.8 hours for teens overall).
- They own or use: cell phone (88 percent), social networking profile (93 percent), Instant Messaging (IM) screen-name (75 percent).
- In the past month they sent e-mail (90 percent), checked out someone else's online profile (88 percent), updated their own online profile (81 percent), posted or viewed photos or videos (83 percent).
- On a public blog or social networking site, they posted: photos of self (80 percent) or friends (66 percent).
- They are about as likely to think personal information online is unsafe (54 percent versus 59 percent for teens overall).
- They were no more concerned about information online having a negative effect on their future (79 percent versus 76 percent for teens overall).
- They were slightly more likely to agree bullying online is easier to get away with than bullying in person (87 percent versus 81 percent for teens overall).

It's hard enough being gay, but when you are a fourteen-year-old and identify yourself as gay and are trying to deal with everyday life, it's even harder. Kenneth James Weishuhn Jr., or K. J. as he was called, was a freshman at South O'Brien High School in northwest Iowa in early 2012, trying to fit in as he negotiated the byways of high school life. It started with being teased by other boys in class about his sexuality after he came out as being gay. If other students didn't join in on the taunts, they ignored them, fearing reprisal.

A Facebook group popped up online, a hate group against homosexuals. Soon K. J.'s friends were added to the group, where anti-gay hate posts against K. J. were being posted. Then the calls came on his cell phone. Although he tried to ignore the calls, letting them go to voicemail after hearing the first few death threats, they were beginning to wear on K. J.

When K. J.'s mother asked him about the phone calls, he made out like it was no big deal, not letting on how much they hurt him and how scared he was. She found out later that the school had warned the boys who were threatening K. J., but the school never contacted her about the situation, so she had no clue how serious it had become.

On April 15, 2012, K. J.'s stepfather walked into the garage and found K. J. hanging, dead. Family members said they would never forget the stepfather's scream when he discovered K. J.'s body.

After local Iowa media wrote about K. J.'s death, national media piped in, including the *Washington Post*,[5] *Huffingon Post*,[6] and *Fox News*.[7] LGBT activists worldwide called for action against cyberbullies, and even superstar Madonna made a point by flashing a photo of K. J. on stage during her European concert tour in late 2012, which was later uploaded as a music video, "Nobody Knows Me."[8]

The last post K. J. made on his personal Facebook profile page[9] on April 3, 2012, was a compilation of photos of him looking happy, healthy, and full of life.

A Facebook group,[10] still active, remembers K. J. as the kind and sensitive soul he was, complete with photos of K. J. and touching posts.

A website at udemy.com[11] notes the following, posted in June of 2014:

"Girls are more likely than boys to be victims or cyberbullies themselves and 34 percent of individuals who have engaged in cyberbullying have also been cyberbullied themselves."

This website also notes seven reasons why teens cyberbully:

1. To show off to friends (11 percent)
2. To be mean (14 percent)
3. Other factors (16 percent)
4. To embarrass another person (21 percent)
5. For fun or entertainment (28 percent)
6. Because they felt the other person deserved it (58 percent)
7. To get back at someone (58 percent)

Nobullying.com goes even further to explain why kids and teens cyberbully:[12]

- Their friends are doing it.
- They want to look cool and fit in.
- They are rebelling against their parents.
- They want to act like adults.

- They are bullies by nature.
- They are seeking attention.
- They want to gain more popularity.

Another reason cyberbullies do what they do is that they feel they can remain anonymous by using a free e-mail account through a site such as Gmail, Hotmail, or Yahoo! Or they create a fake account on social media sites, other websites, or apps, and use those to bully their victims. Some may even go to the extreme of getting a burner cell phone[13] to text and call their victims. What they don't know is that it all can be traced back to them.

Law enforcement or lawyers can subpoena the records from the website or Internet service provider (ISP) in question with the specific day and time of the cyberbullying. A list of IP (Internet protocol) addresses associated with the dates and times provided will be in the subpoena. An IP address is typically four sets of numbers, with one to three numerals in each set, such as 192.254.189.212. That IP address is assigned to one account/person. Every home, office, school, or other setting that has Internet service through an ISP has one IP address assigned to each computer. In cases where Wi-Fi is used, one IP address is used for that building or location.

The ISP would then provide law enforcement or the lawyer with the contact info—who that account belongs to—and it would proceed from there through the legal system.

Cell/smartphones are handled in much the same way, with the number (if known) subpoenaed from the cell phone provider and the contact information given to law enforcement or a lawyer for legal proceedings. Burner phones are a bit harder, but eventually they can be traced back to the store where they were purchased, the transaction identified by the product ID number and how it was paid for. If it was by credit or debit card, the credit card issuer can be subpoenaed to get the contact information of the card owner. If it was cash, it may come down to security camera video footage or "pinging" the phone.

In 2012, the U.S. Court of Appeals for the Sixth Circuit ruled that law enforcement agencies don't need a warrant to "ping" and track prepaid cell phone locations.[14]

So, no one is truly anonymous online. Sometimes this is hard for people using the Internet, especially cyberbullies, to remember, because they get so caught up in making their victim feel bad.

In cases like Amanda Todd's and Kenneth Weishuhn's, they can do it in more ways than just one, such as using Facebook, Twitter, Snapchat, Instagram, e-mail, instant messaging, message boards, sometimes even "snail" mail (postal mail), landline phone calls, cell phone calls and, if they really want to torment their victim, in person.

Stopbullying.gov claims that cyberbullies tend to have parents who are less involved, they are less excited about school, and they are depressed or anxious. Cyberbullies also often have trouble controlling their emotions and impulses and find it hard to follow rules.

The National Council on Crime Prevention reported in a survey of teenagers that 81 percent said they believe others cyberbully because it's funny.[15] They don't see the person face-to-face or hear their voice; all they see is a screen, so they don't realize the harm they are doing. And in many states cyberbullying has consequences beyond possible school suspension or being sued by the victim's parents.

Only when they are caught does reality set in. Many try to backtrack, claiming the victim started it, and they were just defending themselves. Oth-

Richard Guerry, executive director of The Institute for Responsible Online and Cell Phone Communication (IROC2). © Richard Guerry.

ers claim they didn't mean for it to go that far. But in the end, the consequences scare the majority of them. From suspension from school or detention to possible criminal charges that could lead to jail time, those consequences could haunt them for the rest of their life, affect future schooling, jobs, and even relationships.

Richard Guerry, executive director of The Institute for Responsible Online and Cell Phone Communication (IROC2),[16] says this about cyberbullies: "For every child or teen that exhibits the behavior of a cyberbully, I can show you an adult who exhibits similar and sometimes worse behavior setting the wrong example."

He said that in his experience, from being in different communities across the United States and Canada on a daily basis, he often sees cyberbullying occur as a result of the following:

- A heat-of-the-moment, spontaneous venting of frustration about a specific event, another individual's actions, or a social media post. Typically a bully has remorse once emotions have settled down.
- Premeditated bullying based on a dislike for another person, group, or organization (i.e., photo shopping photos, creating false social media profiles and accounts about the victim, etc.)
- Participation in an ongoing group discussion, topic, or post about an unfortunate or controversial situation (piling on or shaming someone who may have had a nude or private picture posted online)

CHAPTER TWO

What Is Cyberbullying?

Jessica Logan, a senior at Sycamore High School in Cincinnati, Ohio, loved her boyfriend, Ryan Salyers. She sent a nude photo of herself from the neck down to him during spring break in 2007, feeling very proud of herself and her eighteen-year-old body. She broke up with him in December 2007 and soon discovered that the private photo she sent to him had been forwarded to more than one hundred students at four different schools. She was understandably upset when students would pass by her in the hallway and call her a "slut," a "whore," and worse. She just couldn't believe Ryan did this to her.

At first she was too ashamed to tell her parents. She tried to go to school but found herself hiding in the bathroom. Mostly, she skipped school because of the bullying and harassment she had to endure.

In May 2008, she decided to do an interview about the bullying with a local TV station, WLWT in Cincinnati.[1] She wanted others her age and their parents to know what happened to her. She wanted to warn them about what could happen if they sexted their boyfriend or girlfriend and then the photo was sent to others besides the person they wanted to share it with.

She told the station's Sheree Paolello that the bullying and harassment didn't just happen at school, but it followed her home or when she went out. At one point during the interview, she burst into tears, saying, "I still get harassed and stuff. I just want to make sure no one else will have to go through this same thing."

The interview, although it blurred her face and changed her voice to keep her anonymity, did not sit well with fellow students. They figured out it was Jessica, and the harassment and bullying only increased. Not only was it at school, it was via text messaging, phone calls, online, and wherever she went.

Two months later, in July 2008, Jessica attended the funeral of a fellow student who had committed suicide. The harassment and bullying targeted at her had continued, and she couldn't deal with it anymore. Her mother found her hanging in her bedroom closet, her cell phone on the floor at her feet.

"Almost eight months later, my daughter is buried in the ground. Are you kidding me? Where were you?" asked Jessica's mother, Cynthia, when she was interviewed by WLWT after her daughter's death.[2] She and her husband were so angry that authorities had done nothing. "The police department didn't protect her. The school didn't protect her. She had no one."

The school resource officer noted that he had tried to do something, but because Jessica was eighteen and considered an adult, he couldn't get charges pressed against the students harassing her. The school superintendent claimed that because a lot of the students were from other schools besides Sycamore High School, nothing could be done. Allegedly, because Jessica took the photo at her home instead of on school grounds, again, nothing could be done.

Jessica's parents decided to take matters into their own hands. On December 2, 2009, Cynthia and Albert Logan filed a federal lawsuit against the city of Cincinnati, the school district, the ex-boyfriend, and several students who had received the nude photo of their daughter.[3]

According to the complaint, "Jessica's grades and attendance at school deteriorated. She had planned to attend the University of Cincinnati after graduation, but her goals were jeopardized by her fear and distress at school. She skipped school because she was too emotionally distraught. Sycamore Schools responded by sending truancy notices and letters to her parents threatening that Jessica would not graduate. Sycamore Schools failed to investigate the harassment, failed to end the harassment, and failed to help Jessica with her emotional turmoil."

Jessica's parents sought punitive damages for discrimination, civil rights violations, privacy invasion, and emotional distress.

It took some time, but finally, in October 2012, Jessica's parents won their lawsuit.[4] They reached a settlement of $154,000 (the original amount was $220,000 minus $66,000 in legal fees). No amount of money would bring back their daughter, but they were comforted by the fact that after the lawsuit was filed, the Jessica Logan Act[5] was sure to pass in Ohio.

And it did, in May 2013. The bill expanded the current anti-bullying law to prohibit harassment by electronic means, which included harassment, intimidation, and bullying through computers, cell phones, or other electronic devices.

One can only hope that Jessica is looking down in approval that something had been done to help other students who were being bullying and harassed.

So, what is cyberbullying? Although technically it is cyberstalking, which is repeated communications online after the harasser has been asked to stop, the media coined the word cyberbullying and attributed it mainly to kids and teens. And the word stuck.

We all know what bullying is—many readers may have been bullied as a child. It meant being teased or harassed at school about anything: the clothes you wore, your hairstyle, if you wore eyeglasses, if you were a "nerd," too smart or not so smart, your family was poor, you were weird. You name it: it could be held against you by other students. Sometimes the bully was older and bigger, sometimes just someone who was nasty and mean to everyone. But at least you could escape the bullying after school, when you went home. Then you had the weekends, school vacation, summer vacation, and holidays to get away from the bullying.

These days with smartphones, tablets, laptops, gaming consoles, and desktop computers, kids and teens can't escape the cyberbullying. They can be texted, contacted on an app, contacted via a social networking site on the Web, during a game they are playing, via e-mail, or just about anywhere online or on their cell phone twenty-four hours a day, seven days a week.

This over-connectedness has been trying, not only for kids and teens, but also for their parents, school faculty, and even law enforcement.

How do you tell a kid or teen to tune out the bullying?

How do you tell him to stay off the Internet or cell phone, to ignore the bully or bullies?

It's nearly impossible.

According to stopbullying.gov, cyberbullying can take many forms, including mean text messages or e-mails, rumors sent by e-mail or posted on social networking sites, and embarrassing pictures, videos, websites, or fake profiles.[6]

The site also notes that cyberbullying messages and images can be posted anonymously and distributed quickly to a very wide audience. It can be difficult, sometimes impossible, to trace the source, especially if the inappropriate or harassing messages, texts, and pictures have been deleted after being viewed.

Although the majority of Internet users surf the Web for entertainment, connecting with friends and family around the world, researching school assignments or posting vacation photos, the Internet and cell phones can also be used to bully and hurt others. It seems that kids and teens are the most affected by this.

The Cyberbullying Research Center conducted a study in 2014 among 661 students ages eleven to fourteen at schools throughout the northeastern United States.[7] They found:

- Cell phones continue to be the most popular technology among adolescents; almost 80 percent of the sample report having used one at least weekly. Social media sites and apps such as Instagram and Snapchat have gained a lot of popularity among middle school students.
- Approximately 35 percent of the students in the sample report experiencing cyberbullying in their lifetimes. When asked about specific types of cyberbullying in the previous thirty days, mean or hurtful comments (14.4 percent) and rumors spread (14.1 percent) online continue to be among the most commonly cited. Eighteen percent of the sample reported being cyberbullied in one or more of the nine types reported, two or more times during the previous thirty days.
- Approximately 17 percent of the students in the sample admitted to cyberbullying others in their lifetimes. Posting mean or hurtful comments and spreading rumors online were the most common types of cyberbullying they reported during the previous thirty days. Six percent of the sample reported cyberbullying using one or more of the nine types reported (only six of the types are displayed in the chart above), two or more times during the previous thirty days.
- Adolescent girls are significantly more likely to have experienced cyberbullying in their lifetimes (40.1 percent versus 29.3 percent). This difference narrows a bit when reviewing experiences over the previous thirty days. Boys are slightly more likely to report cyberbullying others during their lifetime (17.7 percent versus 16.5 percent). The type of cyberbullying tends to differ by gender; girls are more likely to spread rumors whereas boys are more likely to post hurtful pictures or videos.

Some of the stories shared on the Cyberbullying Research Center's website[8] will make you cringe, cry, and curl your toes. They show that this is a worldwide problem and it is not going away:

My sixteen year old son was cyber bullied on Facebook over a period of 8 hours. The event was so traumatic it caused my son to have an acute psychotic break and to be hospitalized in an adolescent psychiatric ward for almost a month. He is changed forever and will never be the same mentally. Internet bullying can hurt and affect people and kids need to know this. These kids are not being punished in any way and think the incident is funny! We know it is life changing. —Parent of 16-year-old boy from Minnesota

I found my daughter was being cyber bullied a week ago. It had started a few weeks earlier but became extreme last week. This was part of an ongoing bullying campaigned by a group of girls at her school after a broken friendship. When it became cyber I kept copies of the harassment which was lucky as I was able to take it to the school. She had been called vile horrible names, accused for things she hadn't done and set up to appear racist. There were threats of bashing. Finally she was provoked and she ended up using language out of character in retaliation. We rang the school who suggested the Police. We rang them and they said that as they are all under 14yrsold they couldn't do much. I then referred to the school policy which clearly stated that if cyber bullying could be directly related to the child and school then it was an issue the school had to deal with in order to create a safe environment for my daughter. Feeling i might be dismissed with "your daughter is too sensitive" or similar I wrote a very precise 3 page letter with 6 attachments cover 22 pages of evidence. Protocol was then followed which was satisfactory. I did however suggest that a very active learning program be set up to educate these children on how to use Facebook and how to change privacy settings etc. I explained that banning this technology was a useless endeavor and would not work so we need to work with it. I would love to be able to do more in the schools so have found your site fantastic. —Parent of 11-year-old girl from Australia

I think that cyber bullying is one of the worst things that a teenager may be exposed to. But in this age kids cannot act properly. The cyberbullies are always not self-confident children who, in many cases, envy their victims. I was bullied twice. The first incident happened 2 years ago in a new social site- Formspring.me In this site you can send your opinion or question anonymously. One person sent me a message claiming that I was fake and that I wasn't a good friend. I was too offended to answer and I just disabled my account. The second incident happened a year ago. Those who I had considered my "best friends" tended to tease me often about my appearance. This teasing eventually led to harsh words exchanged over Facebook, which by a month time resulted in cyber-bullying. The bullying ended when I blocked them, and moved after the school year. So if you are bullied the best thing to do is to block those people or just find a different social network. Don't pay attention to the bullies because most of things they say are not true. However, if the bullying becomes very serious then an adult should be informed or help.—14-year-old boy from USA

When I was 8 years old, I met a girl who had gotten into a fight with me a week later. This resulted in cyber bullying that lasted 5 years. The girl was now 16 and was still harassing me. I told my parents who stopped the messages but then the girls mugged me and attacked me. I was in the hospital for 1 week. The girls were caught by the police and now the girls are in juvenile hall. I'm glad that it stopped.—14-year-old girl from Wales, UK

I went to check my e-mail and there was a message from some people in my old school sent these threatening e-mails some saying "we'll hunt you down at your NEW school and you'll never know what hit you." i felt very scared and at the same time i wondered how they knew my e-mail address. So i told a teacher at that school but then I remembered that at that school they do nothing about this stuff and they are still coming those e-mails.—13-year-old girl from Canada

My best friend and I were so close, we could almost be sisters. We were going on holiday to Scotland in October to take a break from all our crazy work from school, because we both just started an early GCSE. Until she started getting friendly with another girl, who I instantly didn't like, as I thought she was a bad influence. Eventually I started getting nasty texts and emails, and messages on MSN about my appearance and personality. I broke down in tears one night when something about Scotland came on the television. I started getting emotionally depressed at home and at school, and my work was getting effected and my family was deeply alarmed by this. In the end I told her that I wasn't sure if i wanted to go to Scotland with her, so the messages got worse. In the end I showed my parents and teachers. It's not so bad now, even though I still get depressed sometimes, but now I'm sure who my true friends are.—13-year-old girl from England

As you know, Japan has very bad bullying. Cyber bullying, physical bullying, and mental abuse bullying. We have a very high rate of suicide attempts at the age bracket of middle school kids to high school kids. This is a story about a best friend I had who committed suicide right in front of me. And all it started was a crush she had, it was such a small thing. All she wanted to do is have a normal teenage life; that never happened. She wanted to join in the group but everyone called her "gloomy, sullen, creepy." It wasn't very nice at all. The tone of their voices changed when she came in the room, there were thumbnails in her shoes, dead animals in her desk, and many more. There were also a lot of hate mail. Sometimes just to ease the pain I deleted the mails before she could even see them, but that didn't do much good. I wish I could've helped more . . . Every day I saw her eyes die and become darker and darker. It was the time when I was going home with her and we were waiting for the train to pass by; it was that time when she just pushed me away and ran in front of the tracks and committed suicide. Now it has been 3 years since she did this act, I still regret not saving her, I still regret everything I could not have done. —16-year-old girl from Japan

Although no one can delete cyberbullying 100 percent, there are ways to combat it, learn about it, and learn how to deal with it. The following chapters will describe them in more detail.

CHAPTER THREE

~

Cyberbullying Laws

Rehtaeh Parson, from Nova Scotia, was fifteen years old when she tried to kill herself on April 4, 2013. The reason? Photos of her being penetrated during an alleged gang rape while she was vomiting out a window were texted to two people.

This happened in November 2011 when she was with four male friends and became drunk. Soon those photos found their way online. People who saw the photos began calling Rehtaeh a slut, a whore, and worse online.

She was humiliated.

To make matters worse, people sent her e-mails and messages, taunting her about the photo.

Although she reported the photos to the Royal Canadian Mounted Police (RCMP), after a yearlong investigation, they concluded no crime had been committed.

Rehteah felt she couldn't take it anymore, so she locked herself in the bathroom at her home and attempted to hang herself to end her misery. Instead of dying, she ended up in a coma. Her family stayed with her at the hospital as she lay there on life support. They finally reached the hard decision to take her off life support on April 7, 2013, and she passed away.

Suddenly, the RCMP reopened the investigation, claiming it had new information. Charges of child pornography were filed against the photographer and the young man in the photo.

Because no laws in Nova Scotia dealt with online bullying, which happened to Rehtaeh, one of the men involved in posting and texting the photos of the alleged gang rape basically got off with a slap on the wrist during a court hearing on January 15, 2015: twelve months of probation. He also was ordered to refrain from drinking alcohol or making contact with the dead girl's family and to undergo a mental health assessment.

To make matters worse, because Rehtaeh and this young man were both under the age of eighteen when the incident occurred, Canadian law dictated that their names could not be publicized in the media.

Rehtaeh's parents lobbied to have the ban lifted—they wanted people to know Rehtaeh's name and what happened to her in the hope that it wouldn't happen to another teenager.

They got their wish in December 2014, although the young man's name still is protected by that same ban.

At the court hearing on January 15, 2015, Rehteah's mother gave an impact statement on behalf of her daughter.

"Her voice was not heard when she struggled to be heard, but it sure is now," Leah Parsons said. "I was unable to console her as she crumbled emotionally after that photo was taken. The photo set into motion a series of emotional turmoil. She was fifteen years old when that photo started circulating; the cruelty she received would have been too much for an adult to endure, let alone a child."[1]

Gregory Lenehan, the judge, noted that the young man who appeared in the photo with a smiling thumbs up as he raped Rehtaeh "displayed absolutely no respect" for Rehtaeh, instead using her as a prop for his enjoyment.

When the judge was told that the young man in the photo cried when he heard that Rehtaeh had died, the judge told him he should have cried when she was alive.

The man who took the photo was given a conditional discharge, but the judge had harsh words for the young man in the photo, noting that the situation deserved a more severe penalty.

"You lit the wild fire, so to speak, and it got completely out of control," Judge Lenehan said.[2]

In his own defense, the young man had the gall to say, "Humans make mistakes. I will not live with the guilt of someone passing away, but I will live with the guilt of the photo."

He pleaded guilty to one count of distributing child pornography.

Ivan Herritt, a supporter of Rehteah's family who attended the sentencing, was disgusted with the result.

"That kid pled guilty to having sex with her while she was vomiting out a window," he said. "Where's the consent? Where's the rape charge? How do you give consent when you are vomiting out of a window?"[3]

As a result of Rehteah's tragic ending and the cyberbullying she endured, a law called the Cyber-Safety Act was passed in Nova Scotia in May 2013.

However, on December 1, 2015, Justice Glen McDougall of the Supreme Court of Nova Scotia concluded that the law violated the Charter rights to freedom of expression and liberty and he struck it down completely. He claimed the law had been written too broadly, which infringed on a person's rights to liberty.

"I have already found that the act, and in particular the definition of cyberbullying, is overbroad. By casting the net too broadly, and failing to require proof of intent or harm, or to delineate any defences, the act limits the right to liberty in a way that has no connection with the mischief it seeks to address."[4]

Are cyberbullying laws impossible to enact? Can they be enforced once they have been passed or will they, too, go the way of the Nova Scotia law and be struck down? Since the term "cyberbullying" was coined, lawmakers have argued and scrambled to do something about it, mainly because of the media frenzy every time a child commits suicide because he was cyberbullied.

New Jersey is one state that tried to do something about this. In 2014, legislation was passed that would make it mandatory for all middle school students in the Garden State to take classes on how to use social media ethically. It went into effect that school year.

According to Joseph Yeager, a cyber safety advocate,[5] "While many schools already have existing policies in place designed to prevent cyberbullying and encourage positive behavior, students may not even know about the policy. This new law makes it mandatory for all middle school students to actually learn about how their actions can impact others."

Some states have considered laws that would fine a cyberbully anywhere from fifty to one hundred dollars per incident, hoping that putting a dent in the cyberbully's pocket would make him stop.

But will a law like this really make a difference? Who will pay for it? How will it affect the school's current curriculum? Will students learn anything and stop being cyberbullies? No one can answer those questions.

Sometimes the cyberbullying victim has to take the law into her own hands, just as Alex Boston of Cobb County, Georgia, did in 2011. A middle school student at the time, Alex discovered she was the object of a fake Facebook page created using her name. Photos of her were posted so that her face looked fat; posts by "her" claimed she was a racist by linking racist videos to the profile, and said she was a lesbian. More than seventy people became friends with this fake account, and some of her friends confronted

Joseph Yeager, cyber safety advocate. © Joseph Yeager.

her, asking why she was posting such nasty things. After crying in the bathroom at school, Alex went home and told her parents, who were appalled at what they found online.

Her parents contacted school officials. They immediately talked to the two teens who had made the fake profile, Dustin Athearn and Melissa Snodgrass, and got them to admit to creating it. But because the profile had been created off school grounds, school officials said their hands were tied.

Frustrated, Alex's parents kept reporting the fake profile to Facebook, but nothing was done. Alex withdrew, basically crawling into a "shell," just hoping it would go away. Her parents finally went to local police, who filed an incident report. Again, nothing was done.

Although Georgia had a cyberbullying law, it covered what happened *in* the school, not what happened off school grounds. Alex's parents decided to find a lawyer, and after numerous attempts, found two who listened to their story and agreed to take action.

In April 2012, a lawsuit was filed against the two students and their parents, claiming defamation and libel for the false statements posted online and using Alex's identity for the profile that was created on Facebook. Oddly enough, the same week the lawsuit was filed, the fake Facebook profile suddenly disappeared.

Dustin Athearn's parents defended the suit and won on a summary judgment, but that ruling was overturned by an appeals decision dated October 10, 2014.

A three-judge appeals panel noted in their opinion,[6] "Some of these postings were graphically sexual, racist, or otherwise offensive and some falsely stated that Alex was on a medication regimen for mental health disorders and that she took illegal drugs."

The appeals judges also wrote, "During the 11 months the unauthorized profile and page could be viewed, the Athearns made no attempt to view the unauthorized page, and they took no action to determine the content of the false, profane, and ethnically offensive information that Dustin was charged with electronically distributing. They did not attempt to learn to whom Dustin had distributed the false and offensive information or whether the distribution was ongoing. They did not tell Dustin to delete the page. Furthermore, they made no attempt to determine whether the false and offensive information Dustin was charged with distributing could be corrected, deleted, or retracted."

The Cyberbullying Research Center has a list of which U.S. states have or are proposing cyberbullying laws on its website[7] with links to those laws. If you haven't had a chance to peruse it yet, I can tell you it's an eye-opener.

Some argue that all fifty states and many countries already have laws in place to handle cyberbullying, cyberstalking, or related laws.[8]

Cyberstalking is defined by the U.S. Department of Justice[9] as "the use of the Internet, e-mail, or other electronic communications devices to stalk another person. Stalking generally involves harassing or threatening behavior that an individual engages in repeatedly, such as following a person, appearing at a person's home or place of business, making harassing phone calls, leaving written messages or objects, or vandalizing a person's property."

This is what cyberbullies do. So is it necessary to pass cyberbullying laws? Or do schools, parents, and others just need to be educated about cyberbullying and how to deal with it if it does happen?

If a cyberbullying situation gets out of control, as Rehteah's did, why aren't authorities using laws that are already on the books, if they are available? Many argue it is due to lack of education among law enforcement. Many law enforcement agencies don't take cyberstalking cases seriously and tell victims to "stay off the Internet," which is not the answer. You don't tell a stalking victim to stay in the house, do you?

Others simply don't know how to handle an online-related case. Then you have the authorities who are on the ball, but when they get to court, they get a judge who doesn't "get" how someone can be stalking or bullied online and dismisses the case.

It's a typical catch-22: round and round we go.

To protect kids and teens from cyberbullies, they must have recourse if they become victims. If they have no recourse, the cyberbullies feel emboldened; their ego is inflated, knowing they can get away with hurting someone online (and sometimes offline). Then they cyberbully someone else, and who knows where it will end?

If not a law, then schools, parents, and other adults need to take action. They certainly don't want to see a student or their child become the next Rehteah Parsons, and neither does the public.

Joseph Yeager sums it up well: "Personally, I think specific laws are really meant to appease the special interest groups that ask for them. They should be covered by other, existing laws. Similarly, do we need additional laws that cover assault for hate crimes when assault itself is already illegal? One thing they might want to do is increase the number of laws that were violated, allowing for increased punishment. However, since very few cyberbullying crimes ever make it to a court room, how effective is that really?"[10]

CHAPTER FOUR

Are Schools Ready for Cyberbullies?

Scott Smith of Belfountain, Ontario, Canada, had always been a go-getter. When he was nine years old, he wanted to raise money for Somalian relief and started his own charity. He raised $3,400. Even with this ambitious endeavor, he couldn't get away from the bullying he received at school. He was teased, bullied, and punched because he had Asperger's syndrome, a form of autism.[1]

"They called me stupid and retarded," recalled Scott.[2] "This happened from the beginning in kindergarten right up to the fifth grade. The worst was when I was on the computer on a website called Bitstrips.[3] Two boys from my class made a comic strip that was supposed to make fun of me during Thanksgiving at my mom's house. One of them was supposed to be my best friend, and it really hurt."

Instead of taking the abuse or running away from it, Scott decided to start an anti-bullying club he called "No Bullying Today" at his school. He enlisted two good friends and the principal of Belfountain Public School, where he attended classes.

Some 250 students attended the school, and on average, forty would attend the anti-bullying club meetings.

Scott's dad, Steve, was proud of him for standing up for himself and others.

Local media caught wind of the club, and Ontario's minister of education wrote to Scott, praising him for what he had done. The press attention attracted champion pro golfer Ernie Els, who supported the cause and even devoted a page on his website about Scott.[4]

A website for the "No Bullying Today" club was made, two hundred T-shirts were sold, and every student at the school signed a pledge not to be a bully, online or offline. They even had their own motto, "Don't stand by, stand up."

Other schools around the world inquired of Scott how to start their own clubs, and Scott was happy with the results. But, before he left the sixth grade, a new principal was hired who disbanded the club, including the website.

"He did not care about the anti-bullying club and did nothing to help. That made me very frustrated," Scott said.[5] "He got rid of it when I left school."

This didn't deter Scott at his new school—"I joined my new school's social justice club put brilliantly together by my vice president."

Although it is not surprising, it is a shame the new principal of Scott's former school disbanded the anti-bullying club and took down the website. It is more than a bit disheartening, as it is not an uncommon practice for administrators to stick their heads in the sand like ostriches and ignore a growing problem that is not going away.

For example, I am asked to speak at many schools about cyberbullying and how to deal with it. When I give a presentation to students, I do a lot of research beforehand, with the permission of whoever books me for that school. This means using an alter ego—a teen boy or girl—on Facebook or the most popular social media platform in use at that time. I access online records of the school's sports team members and honor roll students. I ask students at that school to be my friend, follower, or whatever term they use and see how many accept me, a complete stranger, to their list. I do not interact with them—if they message me asking how they know me, I make note of that, but I do not respond. Astoundingly, on average, more than 90 percent of the students accept my alter ego to their list.

I then go through their posts, comments, photos, and videos as well as their account information. Here I am, a complete stranger, now with access to their e-mail address, Skype or other screen name, cell and sometimes home phone numbers, where they work after school, their class schedule, home address, and more.

When I give my presentation at the school, I show how many accepted a complete stranger, how many of them posted their personal information (but I do not show that information), some risqué posts, and then I show them photos (with their faces blacked out) of them giving the finger, drinking alcohol, smoking cigarettes and sometimes marijuana, in sexually provocative poses and more that should never have been on their social media account.

You can hear a pin drop at this point in my presentation.

One school I went to a few years back wanted me to speak to students during the day, then to parents that night.

I went in, did my presentation, gently chastised them for what they posted, especially a group someone started titled "I hate Mr. (blank)," one of the teachers. I told them not to do this, because they will be caught and punished. The vice principal, who had booked me, thanked me and said it was exactly what the students needed to see and hear.

As I was packing up my laptop, the vice principal said the principal wanted to see me in her office. I thought she was going to thank me as well.

When I sat down in a chair across from the principal's desk, I was handed a check and told not to bother showing up for the presentation for parents that night. The principal said that the teacher with whom the group had been angry was very upset that I had showed it in the presentation (not considering the fact that *anyone* on Facebook could see this group) and was afraid parents would be coming to the presentation with "pitchforks," angry with me.

At first I was too shocked to say anything. Then, bluntly, I told the principal that the teacher needed to grow a backbone because this kind of thing was going to get worse before it got better. I graciously offered to give the parent presentation in the fall if she still wanted me to do it, because I had already been paid for it. She accepted, but the school never called.

Not long after, a huge scandal rocked the school. It was spread all over the media, both local and national.

The *Portland Press Herald* in Maine reported[6] "two players face each other, smiling, and give the Nazi salute with one arm in the air, while a third player sits cross-legged between them, holding her hands in peace signs. All three are wearing their team uniforms."

It was all I could do not to call the school and say, "I told you so."

Savannah Dietrich was sixteen years old in August 2011, doing what most teens do on lazy, hot summer nights—hanging out with friends and partying. Although she knew she shouldn't, she partook in the alcohol that was flowing freely around the campfire, doing shots with friends and having a good time. But when she woke up the next morning, she knew something was wrong. She was hungover and couldn't remember much of what had happened the night before. She shrugged it off and for months tried to ignore the smothered laughter from fellow students in the hallways of her Louisville, Kentucky, high school.

When she learned what had happened, she was mortified. Two sixteen-year-old boys from her school had taken advantage of her when she passed out. They pulled down her bra and took cell phone photos, put their fingers in her vagina and sexually assaulted her, then took even more photos. They quickly circulated around the school. All she could think about was how many people had seen them, and who they were.

She told her parents, who reported it to the Louisville Metro Police Department. The two boys were charged with felony sexual abuse and misdemeanor voyeurism. And they couldn't even consider pleading not guilty—their faces were clearly visible in the photographs each had taken of the other.

At a hearing on June 26, 2012, the prosecutor opted for lenience in exchange for the boys' guilty pleas. In addition, the court ordered Savannah not to talk about the outcome or risk 180 days in jail and a fine of five hundred dollars.

Not happy with what basically amounted to a slap on the wrist, Savannah tweeted,[7] "There you go, lock me up" to her couple of hundred Twitter followers. She followed that tweet with the full names of the boys who had sexually assaulted her, then finished with, "I'm not protecting anyone that made my life a living Hell."

The attorneys representing the two boys wanted Savannah to be held in contempt of court. When the media got wind of this, a firestorm broke out. A petition was started on change.org, and in one day, more than sixty-two thousand signatures in support of Savannah outing her accusers were posted online.

On July 23, 2012, the boys' attorneys withdrew their motion to have Savannah held in contempt of court. That September, a judge ruled that all documents pertaining to her case were to be made public, including the names of the boys who assaulted her.

The two boys were sentenced in October 2012—each to fifty hours of community service, and to undergo sexual assault counseling. They were also told that when they reached the age of nineteen, they could file motions to have their cases dismissed and their guilty pleas withdrawn, thereby expunging their criminal records.

Although that may seem like little relief to Savannah, she didn't back down when she saw that her attackers were pretty much getting away with what they did to her. She fought back, and her courage should give all cyberbullying victims the courage to fight back.

When asked if schools are handling cyberbullying well, Dr. Justin W.

Patchin, codirector of the Cyberbullying Research Center, was ambivalent: "Some are, some aren't. It really depends on the situation and the school, but there certainly are many examples of what not to do in the media."

One school, Monteagle Elementary School in Monteagle, Tennessee, has a wonderful cyberbullying policy.[8]

It notes rights and responsibilities, such as, "At school it is everyone's responsibility to take the necessary steps to stop bullying behavior. Our school will not tolerate any action that undermines a person's right to feel safe, respected, and to learn. This policy addresses conduct taking place on school grounds, at any school-sponsored activity, or outside school (if the bullying disrupts the school learning environment or possibly poses an imminent threat to the safety of any student)."

The policy notes the different types of bullying that occur, how to report it, intervention, investigation, and discipline (punishment).

It is a good policy that other schools can use as the basis for their own policies.

Monteagle Elementary also formed a "Bully Prevention Taskforce," consisting of school employees, parents, and students, which educates students about bullying, discusses bullying-related issues and problems, and provides events to promote anti-bullying.

Other schools have events such as cyberbullying poster contests, plays, making videos or ads about cyberbullying, and more. All it takes is a little imagination, prizes donated by local businesses, and cyberbullying awareness can be a huge hit!

Some schools bring in an expert such as Josh Chin, managing director of Netforce.[9]

"When asked by parents or principals of schools, I engage both students and parents in a dialogue on what is cyberspace, what is cyberbullying, and how to approach it," Chin noted. "Traditionally, we think we live in brick and mortar homes. However, with the advent of the Internet, our homes are more like glass homes. Smartphones, webcams, iPads, baby monitors, Facebook, Instagram, etc. enable individuals around the globe to participate in our lives vicariously. I teach students tips, tricks, and try to help them to think twice before posting. My first slide in my presentation has a Spiderman quote: 'With great power comes great responsibility.'"

Most experts agree on one thing: some schools "get it" and have cyberbullying policies in place to try to curb it and deal with it on a case-by-case basis, whereas other schools continue to ignore it. That leaves it up to students like Scott Smith to take matters into their own hands and do something about it.

Or, as Stopcyberbullying.org puts it best,[10] "When schools try and get involved by disciplining the student for cyberbullying actions that took place off-campus and outside of school hours, they are often sued for exceeding their authority and violating the student's free speech right. They also, often lose. Schools can be very effective brokers in working with the parents to stop and remedy cyberbullying situations. They can also educate the students on cyberethics and the law. If schools are creative, they can sometimes avoid the claim that their actions exceeded their legal authority for off-campus cyberbullying actions. We recommend that a provision is added to the school's acceptable use policy reserving the right to discipline the student for actions taken off-campus if they are intended to have an effect on a student or they adversely affect the safety and well-being of student while in school. This makes it a contractual, not a constitutional, issue."

One final note about Scott Smith: Scott got the recognition he so greatly deserved in July 2015 when he was presented with a certificate from the Hudson County Chiefs of Police Association:

> The Hudson County Chiefs of Police Association presents this Certificate of Recognition to Master Scott Smith of Ontario, Canada in recognition of his selfless service and dedication to the cause of Anti-bullying, an issue today that plagues our youth all over the world. Master Smith has set a fine example for other youth and his efforts have not gone unnoticed by police agencies worldwide, including here in the United States of America. By the authority vested in me, as President of the organization, I hereby declare this year's National Night Out in Crime Prevention, being held by the Stevens Police Department, in Hoboken, New Jersey, U.S.A. on August 4th, 2015 to be Scott Smith Day.

Scott Smith. © Steve Smith.

005 Scott Smith, left, and his father, Steve Smith. © Steve Smith.

CHAPTER FIVE

What If Your Child Is a Cyberbully?

No parents want to think that their child can be so cruel as to bully another child, especially when it escalates to cyberbullying.

When United Kingdom native James (pseudonym), sixteen, was home alone while his mother worked, he trolled the Internet out of boredom. One site that caught his eye was Ask.fm,[1] which allows users to ask questions of other users anonymously. What began as a bit of fun soon turned him into a cyberbully.

"The feeling of not having to worry about people knowing who you are is powerful and addictive," James said.[2] "I found myself resorting to abusing others when I was bored, upset, lonely, or angry. It made me feel like I was important and influential in people's lives, even though what I was prompting them to do was negative."

He was asking people why they were so ugly, or they were worthless and didn't deserve to live, among other things. He felt empowered and in no time became addicted to cyberbullying.

But things changed when he began reading stories about teens who had committed suicide because of what cyberbullies were doing to them online. Many were close to his age, and one story in particular hit home—the death of Hannah Smith.[3]

Hannah participated on Ask.fm quite a bit, asking questions about eczema, from which she suffered. She found herself getting answers that were nasty, demeaning, and bullying instead of being compassionate or helpful. It got so bad that on August 9, 2013, she hung herself in her home in Leicestershire, England.

After reading about Hannah's death, James deleted his Ask.fm account and began to apologize to the people he had bullied online.

His mother didn't punish him when she found out he had been cyber-bullying others. Instead, she listened to him when he told her what he'd done and got him involved in after-school events.

"I feel like a lot of weight has been taken off my shoulders since I con-fessed what I had done to those involved," James claimed.[4]

So, what do you do if your child is a cyberbully?

First, let's start with some warning signs:[5]

- When you approach, your child will change what's on his computer screen or smartphone or quickly close whatever he is viewing.
- He will turn off his smartphone or place it upside down so you cannot see what is on the screen.
- He will use his computer or smartphone frequently and/or at all hours of the night.
- He will get annoyed if he doesn't have access to a computer or smartphone.
- He will avoid talking about what he does on the computer or smartphone.
- He will laugh excessively while online or when using his smartphone.
- He will have multiple online accounts or accounts that are not his.
- He has been involved in bullying incidents at school or has been the target of bullies in the past.

Sometimes parents get fed up with the things their children do online. One mother, Cara Schneider, from North Carolina, had tried everything to punish her daughter for cyberbullying, including grounding her, taking away privileges, and having her do chores around the house. When she caught her daughter cyberbullying again in January 2014, she took matters into her own hands.

Cara made her daughter, Hailey, handwrite a sign, took a photo of Hailey holding the sign along with her beloved iPod, then posted the photo on her Facebook profile. The sign read:

My name is Hailey. I am a kind, caring smart girl, but I make poor choices with social media. I am selling my iPod and will be donating the money to charity Beat Bullying in hopes of changing my behavior as well as bringing awareness to bullying. Because bullying is wrong.

One of Cara's Facebook friends shared the photo and post on the website Reddit, where it soon went viral. Not everyone agreed with her parenting choice, but she didn't care. And some were extremely supportive of what she did.

"I'm not worried about the negative that has been said about her punishment," she wrote on her Facebook page.[6] "I am her mother and I did what I thought was best given the circumstances. I've tried other punishments, and this fit the crime. I don't regret a thing."

Although this may seem drastic to some people, sometimes you need to take measures like this to impress on your child that what she does online can have negative consequences.

If you discover your child is a cyberbully, it does not mean you are a bad parent. On the contrary, if you are reading this, it means you want to know how to handle it before it escalates, if it hasn't already. You may feel embarrassed or angry both at yourself and your child. This is not unusual.

Sit your child down and ask why she is cyberbullying others. Let her know you want to help. Don't get angry, don't yell, and don't threaten punishment (at least, not right away).

You may find out your child was or is a victim of a bully and began cyberbullying to counteract it. She may be bored, like James was. Or maybe something at home made her strike out at others online.

Once you find out why she is cyberbullying, let her know that it could lead to legal action, maybe even an arrest by law enforcement if she does not stop. All fifty states and many countries have cyberstalking or online-related laws that can be used in a cyberbullying situation. The first offense is usually a misdemeanor; the second, a felony. Does she really want a criminal record for the rest of her life?

Mike Dreiblatt, president of standuptobullying.net, offers more advice: "Before your child even has a cellphone, talk to them when they're three, four or five years old about what we do online. Like you'd prepare them for crossing the street, prepare them for the digital highway. Kids try on different personalities. A child might try out cyberbullying behavior. You need to tell them, 'That's not how we act in this family, and we mean it.' You almost have to have a family intervention. Tell them, 'We're going to monitor you, and add software so you can't do it.' It's important that this is not yelling at a child, but talking to them and following up."

According to Webroot,[7] bullies often end up with a criminal record.

A study conducted in Finland found that:

- Nearly 60 percent of boys who researchers classified as bullies in grades six to nine were convicted of at least one crime by the age of twenty-four.

Mike Dreiblatt, president of standuptobullying.net. © Mike Dreiblatt.

- Forty percent of them had three or more convictions by age twenty-four.

Your child may get kicked out of school, the victim's parents might take him to court, or he could lose his after-school job because of what he is doing online to others. In addition, he could lose a scholarship or admission to college or university if it comes out that he was cyberbullying.

Your child needs to know that his actions online today can and will affect his future. Anything he posts or does online is there *forever*.

If you don't know the website or app he is using, take time to learn about it. Ask him how to use it—kids and teens love to show off their knowledge, and you will learn something as well.

You may want to sit down with the school counselor, your child's teacher, and/or the principal and let them know what is happening. Your child needs to know from someone besides you that cyberbullying is not a good thing to do.

You also need to mete out some sort of punishment. Experts advise that any computer your child uses (desktop, laptop, or tablet) needs to be in a common room, not in her bedroom where she can close the door and you will not know what she is doing. You may want to consider getting filtering or monitoring software for computers and smartphones.[8] As long as your child is under your roof, and you are paying for the Internet and cell phone use, you have every right to know what she is doing online, texting, and so forth. It is not an infringement of her rights but keeping her safer from cyberbullying and being a cyberbully herself.

You also may want to limit her online time by setting a cutoff time at night. Further, put her smartphone, tablet, and/or laptop in a safe or somewhere she can't get at them. Nothing is so important that she needs to be online or texting at all hours of the night. It can wait until morning.

You need to have your child remove, as best he can, anything he has posted online that would be considered cyberbullying. If some of his friends are involved, ask them to remove those posts as well. If need be, you should talk to the friends' parents to let them know what is happening and how you are trying to help your child stop the cyberbullying. It may be enlightening to the other parents!

One of the hardest things your child will need to do is apologize to those she is cyberbullying. The victim may not want to hear the apology in person, but sending a handwritten or typed letter, which your child has signed, may be the best approach.

Visit some informative websites with your child. NetSmartz[9] has activities and videos appropriate for your child's age. Another great site is ThinkUKnow Australia,[10] which offers information for parents and kids/teens. Its videos are definite eye-openers.

You may want to search online for cyberbullying victims such as Megan Meier,[11] Phoebe Prince,[12] and Tyler Clementi.[13] Unfortunately, the Web has many stories like theirs, but having your child read these stories should change his mind about being a cyberbully.

You don't want your child to be a cyberbully when he grows up, do you? It will be hard for you to carry out these steps if you discover your child is a cyberbully, but in the long run, it may save a cyberbullying victim's life.

~

CHAPTER SIX

Cyberbullying Victims
Who Fought Back

In 2010, Carter Isaac of Turner,[1] Maine, was in the sixth grade at Turner Elementary School. He was different from the other kids—he liked to wear sweaters to school and styled his hair unlike everyone else. This led to teasing, then to bullying.

"They used to call me gay and other names that mean the same thing, "Carter recalls. "Soon they started to attack other things about me. For example, people started to tell me music made me lame and uncool and I should stop. My friends even started to distance themselves from me because they didn't want to be associated with the bullying."

His grandfather, Ron Landry,[2] had no clue at the time.

"Imagine my pride, when my grandson Carter, at five years old, started playing the piano, and before too long was way beyond his years," he gushed. An accomplished musician, he showed great promise. As he continued to awe his teachers, he began writing music at ten years of age.

Carter tried to fit in at school and began cutting his hair a different way and dressed more like the other kids, but he hated it. He even stopped anything to do with music.

"People were anonymously commenting only that my music was bad," Carter said. "They were trying to bring down my accomplishments."

"Carter announced that he would no longer take piano lessons or play music," Ron remembered. "He admitted he was being made fun of because he was a musician and what he looked like, and he had had enough."

But the bullying didn't stop. He was afraid to tell anyone lest he be called a tattletale, although one of his best friends told a teacher, who then reported it to the principal. But nothing was ever done.

Carter Isaac. © Carter Isaac.

Carter kept his head down, did his schoolwork, and tried to ignore the bullying. When his grandfather found out about the bullying, he introduced Carter to Ed Boucher, who owned a recording studio and was a longtime musician.

Carter reluctantly played some of his music for Ed, who was wowed by Carter's talent. He encouraged Carter to continue with his music and planted the idea of writing a song about his bullying experience.

He recorded "Peace Song." Then Carter wrote and recorded "This Is My

Prayer," which recounted how he felt when he was bullied, and that song was put out on a CD.

"I wanted to help others going through the same thing to realize they aren't alone in the matter and that it's okay to be different," Carter says. "Be true to yourself and realize that there are always others to support you."

THIS IS MY PRAYER
—Carter Isaac

Do you think that I can't hear,
What is said when I'm not near?
I'll always stand tall and proud,
One day I'll stand out in the crowd.

Doesn't matter what you wear,
Or even how you do your hair.
We are all the same inside,
I don't want to have to hide.
Will you please stop hurting me,
Filling me with memories,
I never want to see again—
This is my prayer, Amen.

Sometimes I feel so small and afraid,
With no one to come to my aid,
Why do you think that I don't belong?
Do you think I did something wrong?

Doesn't matter what you wear,
Or even how you do your hair.
We are all the same inside,
I don't want to have to hide.
Will you please stop hurting me,
Filling me with memories,
I never want to see again-
This is my prayer, Amen.

I'm laying on the cold hard ground,
With everybody looking down.
It just takes one to break away,
Grab my hand, show them the way.

Doesn't matter what you wear,
Or even how you do your hair.
We are all the same inside,
I don't want to have to hide.
Will you please stop hurting me,
Filling me with memories,
I never want to see again—
This is my prayer, Amen.

His grandfather was watching a local television show one day when the guest was Jim Mayer, aka "Uncle Jim," who was the bass player for Jimmy Buffett's Coral Reefer Band.

Uncle Jim talked about his crusade to eliminate bullying in schools. When he was playing in the band, he was traveling across the country with his anti-bullying message. He said in the interview that if anyone had a bullying story to share, he should e-mail him. Uncle Jim was scheduled to appear at the Bath, Maine, high school the next evening to spread his message.

"Given my range of emotions with Carter's experience, following the broadcast, I e-mailed Jim with Carter's story," Ron said. "I was amazed that within minutes I got a response asking if Jim could meet Carter and hear his song. Obviously, with great delight, I sent Jim an Mp3 of Carter's song 'This Is My Prayer.' Again, within minutes, I had a request asking if Carter could come to Bath the next evening and perform with Jim on stage."

That was the first time Carter ever played for a live audience. Understandably nervous—not only to meet Jim, but also to play live—Carter didn't know how the students in the audience would react to his song. His worries were unfounded; they loved the song, and soon Carter was appearing with Uncle Jim at events throughout New England, playing his song and helping Jim spread the word about bullying and cyberbullying.

(The author of this book and her Cyber Crime Dog, Phoebe [a Siberian husky], made a few appearances with Jim and Carter in Maine and Massachusetts. Phoebe would do some tricks for the audience [double high five, fist bump, and when I asked her, "What do you say to cyberbullies?," she would growl]; then I would talk about WHO@-KTD[3] and how kids and teens could stay safer online.)

Jim was so impressed with Carter's talent that he signed Carter to a contract to write twenty-four songs. Carter wrote them in record time. As of this writing, nothing has happened with them yet, but who knows what the future holds?

The Veayo Twins Trio: Carter Isaac, left; Katherine Veayo, middle; and Kristen Veayo, right.
© Tim Sullivan (facebook.com/TimSullivan).

In 2013, Carter met the Veayo twins, sisters who played and sang songs about their own bullying and cyberbullying experiences.

Kristen and Katherine Veayo were bullied at school when they were eight years old. When they were in high school, they finally switched to another school, hoping the bullying would stop. Although it died down a bit, they were still experiencing it online as well as offline, mainly on Facebook for Katherine.

"Most of the time, I knew exactly who was bullying me because they did it to my face," Kristen recalled.[4] "I'm sure some of them, earlier in my experiences (who were my friends at the time) didn't realize they were doing wrong by me, and thought they were joking around. But that wasn't the case for me—it bothered me, and I was afraid to tell them to stop."

For Kristen, the online bullying happened on several social media sites including AOL Instant Messenger, Formspring.com,[5] and Tumblr,[6] or on her cell phone.

"On AOL, sometimes I would get harassing messages trying to bully me to send pictures of myself (which I never did)," Kristen said. "On Formspring, I would get anonymous messages about me as a person, calling me names like 'whore,' etcetera, which eventually led me to delete my account. I used Tumblr to express my feelings (an outlet for me), and I received a backlash from a group of people who recognized incidents I wrote about as events that

Katherine Veayo. © Katherine Veayo.

linked to me. That as well caused me to delete that account. On my cell phone, I would get mean texts from unknown numbers, and a couple of anonymous calls from people who made fun of me solely on the fact that they thought I was an emo[7] and a 'slut.'"

If that wasn't bad enough, the physical bullying took a toll on the twins.

"Some of the senior boys smashed my head against a locker or shoved me into a locker when I would be in the hallway getting ready for class," Katherine said.[8] "When I would sit down for lunch, my friend group would purposely migrate to a different table or would not leave an available seat for me, so I would have to sit in the music room to eat. I was mostly teased

Kristen Veayo. © Kristen Veayo.

because of my stuttering problem, so whenever I would open my mouth to talk people would laugh at me even before I had anything to say."

Kristen had similar experiences. "I was afraid to walk through the halls because oftentimes I would hear comments, be shoved around as others walked by, and even tripped down the stairs by upperclassmen. This type of bullying was the most painful, and life-changing for me, because I knew what people were capable of doing."

She began to cut herself as a way to deal with the bullying.

"When I was first experiencing bullying, I did not say anything to anyone," Katherine added. "I was worried that it would create more drama than there already was, and I was afraid about what the bullies would do if they found out. When it came to Facebook, I did tell my mother, and she spoke with the girl's mother that had attacked me."

They, like Carter, turned to music as an outlet for their frustration and anger at being bullied. They posted videos of their songs online, and that's when Susan Broude, a producer for a documentary called *Bullied to Silence*,[9] found them. Susan was touched by their music lyrics and wanted the twins to share their story in the documentary, which showcased teens who had been bullied and cyberbullied and did something positive as a result of their experiences.

The twins played their music at schools, festivals, and fairs; and when they met Carter in 2013, it was like a match made in heaven.

"The twins and I met at an anti-bullying rally we were both playing at," Carter remembered. "They needed a keyboard player, and our parents ended up having us play together because our messages were the same. We all focused on writing songs about our experiences with bullying to help others, which made us a perfect match for each other."

Katherine likes to talk about some of the places where they have played.

"We did a show at Cony High School (in Augusta, Maine), and that was a really touching experience for me. A lot of the kids came up to us after the show and shared their experiences, some of them crying and thanking us for what we do. We always feel so blessed to send our message out to the world and to try to help others who are going through or have been through the same things as us."

"Normally, we go into a school and talk about the effects of bullying and how to deal with it," Kristen added. "But we also do other stuff like festivals, restaurant gigs, TV shows (when the opportunity arises), and other stuff. We went to the Bahamas and played at the Hard Rock in Nassau when we were on vacation there. We have slowed a little, due to college being in session—our big crazy music schedules usually happen in the summer."

"At their anti-bullying shows, the message is always the same, 'Bullying comes in many forms,'" Carter's grandfather, Ron, notes. "Cyberbullying is as damaging as any other form of bullying."

When asked what advice he could give kids or teens who are being cyberbullied, Carter responded, "If you are being cyberbullied, alert an adult you trust. They will be able to rectify the matter. If things persist, close down your social media accounts on which the bullying is taking place, or block the people who instigate the bullying. People hiding behind computer screens feel more powerful when they aren't saying things face-to-face—don't give them the power they want."

Truer words were never more appropriate.

His grandfather adds his own advice for cyberbullying victims:

- Do not let anyone define who *you* are.
- Speak up for yourself and/or for a friend.
- Don't be embarrassed, and seek help if you need it.
- *You* are special, regardless of what others say.
- Harmful words can never be taken back.

All three of the now-named Veayo Twins Trio[10] are in college and hopefully will have a very successful future.

"I am going to college for secondary education in English, hopefully with plans to teach English as a second language to French students," Carter enthused. "I am still playing music with the Veayo Twins as well as on my own, and am involved heavily in my school's music program as well."

SCREAM AT WALLS[11]

—Kristen Veayo

If only you knew our lives, my world
then maybe, you would understand how cruel the things they do

Cause being different, it isn't easy
everything goes wrong, and I don't belong
so I go home and I scream at walls
Cause no one understands but me
But me

Being pushed to the limit and shredded into pieces
that's how it feels to be us
the worst is when you're holding the agony inside

Cause being different, it isn't easy
everything goes wrong, and I don't belong
so I go home and I scream at walls
Cause no one understands but me
But me

Lets find our way through the everlasting storm
you'll find your way if you keep your form
Lets find our way through the everlasting storm
we'll find our way whatever it takes

Cause being different, it isn't easy
everything goes wrong, and I don't belong
so I go home and I scream at walls
Cause no one understands but me
But me
But me

CHAPTER SEVEN

When Sexting Becomes Sextortion

Mary Stone[1] (pseudonym) and her boyfriend, Mark Allen[2] (pseudonym) were teens in love in 2007. She was seventeen, he was twenty-three. They loved to chat with other couples via their computer webcam. Sometimes the conversations were sexually charged, leading to one or both couples kissing, fondling, and sexual intercourse on camera.

Mary and Mark discovered that one couple they'd chatted with had video-taped them without their knowledge and posted the video on various porno-graphic websites.

"We were young and didn't even think of anyone videoing us," Mark said. "We were just having fun. We drafted a DMCA[3] (copyright infringement) notice, sent it to the websites that posted the video, and most of them took the video down."

Years went by; Mary and Mark married and moved to Canada. In April of 2015, Mary and Mark heard from relatives that the sexual video of them was being e-mailed or sent via Facebook to their relatives.

"We were afraid that whoever was doing this will post it on websites again," Mark sighed. "We contacted lawyers, but they wanted $400 an hour to help us. We just don't have that kind of money."

This is not an isolated example. In 2007 this might not have been called sexting, but it was a form of it. Almost always it comes down to an innocent act, being young and thinking nothing will ever happen to you, then finding out that it can and will happen—and years down the road, it can crop up again.

Susie Smith[4] (pseudonym), fifteen years old, actively used Kik, a social media app[5] that allows users to connect with friends, family, and strangers who also use the app. From posts to photos to videos, users can do just about anything with Kik on their smartphone.

In February of 2015, Susie got a private message on Kik from someone she did not know.

"He wrote that he had a nude picture of me and threatened to send it to my parents and post it on his account if I didn't do everything he wanted," Susie recalled. "He said he hacked my phone and sent the picture to some of my friends so that I would know that he wasn't joking."

He wasn't. Her friends let her know about the photo.

"I asked him to delete it, but he wouldn't," Susie said. "He messaged me and told me he was gonna track me down and rape me after school."

She didn't even think of going to the police—this complete stranger threatened to unleash the nude photo online everywhere he could if she reported it to them.

But she did report it to Kik, who told her how to block strangers from contacting her, and she deleted the stranger's account. She didn't hear from him again.

Sadly, this is becoming a regular occurrence all over the world, with far worse results than threatening to send the photos or videos to family and friends. Often, the victims are blackmailed for more nude photos and videos, even blackmailed for money.

Interpol notes[6] that "an agent/blackmailer will assume the identity of an attractive man or woman to engage a victim. After gaining their trust, the agent will record footage of the victim performing a sexual act, which they threaten to circulate amongst the victim's friends or post on the Internet unless an amount of money is paid, typically ranging from USD 500 to USD 15,000."

When asked where sexting targets come from, Interpol stated that the majority of countries are those where English is the primary Internet language, such as the United Kingdom, United States, Australia, Singapore, Hong Kong, Indonesia, and Malaysia. They also see similar crimes emerging in French-speaking Africa, targeting France.

In October 2015, three men were charged with threatening young girls if they did not continue to send nude photos to the men:

Nicholas Kurtz, twenty-one, of Clearcreek Township, Ohio, allegedly used Skype to convince several teenage girls to expose themselves to him online. He told one fourteen-year-old girl he would rape and kill her if she wouldn't continue to do what he wanted. He pleaded not guilty to coercion and enticement.

Cody Lee Jackson, twenty, convinced a fourteen-year-old girl via Facebook to come to his apartment in Norwood, Ohio, for sex. He paid for the taxi ride. He couldn't leave his apartment because he was on electronic monitoring for an abduction case. He talked her into moving into his apartment and got her pregnant. His hearing was scheduled for August 2015 for his original abduction case, but before then he left Ohio. This didn't stop him from calling the girl and threatening to kill her and her family if she didn't take nude photos of herself and send them to him via Facebook. He was finally arrested in October 2015 and charged with multiple state and federal counts.

The third man, Bryan Harris, twenty-seven, of Blue Ash, Ohio, sought nude photos from young women on Facebook and other social media websites and apps. If they didn't comply by sending more photos after the initial ones, he threatened to go to their parents or the police. He pleaded not guilty to two counts of coercion and enticement.

The stories just keep coming. It's so easy to find them—just search online for sextortion or sexting, and you'll see far too many stories like those three. Luckily, all of those victims are alive. But some just cannot deal with it and kill themselves. And victims are not always girls.

Daniel Perry lived in Scotland. Seventeen years old, he was a fun-loving teen. Pictures of him online show him with a huge smile, kissing a dolphin. He loved the Internet, like most teens, and was into chatting with people from around the world via Skype,[7] a Web chat site and app. He was shy, so he usually chatted via microphone and not via his webcam.

One day in early 2013, he began chatting with a girl close to his age. They talked about everything and anything. After getting to know her, and she him, she talked him into having an explicit chat with him, filled with sexual innuendo. He felt he knew her well, so he wasn't so shy anymore and gladly went along with it.

Not long after, she demanded money from him—if he didn't pay up, she was going to send a copy of their chat to his parents and maybe the police where he lived. Daniel was distraught, scared, and angry. He refused to pay the money. "She" taunted him.

"I will make you suffer."

"Commit suicide now."

"Are you dead yet?"

In July of 2014, he couldn't deal with it anymore. He leaped to his death from the Forth Road Bridge, just outside of Edinburgh.

"The manner of Daniel's death is every parent's worst nightmare," Nicola

Perry, his mother, said.[8] "After being targeted by complete strangers online, he was left so traumatized by his ordeal that he chose to take his own life. They didn't care that he was a loving and caring person with his whole life ahead of him. To them, he was just another faceless victim to exploit for cash."

Authorities investigated and traced the Skype calls back to Manila in the Philippines. Eight Filipinos were arrested in August 2014 as a result of Operation Strikeback[9] conducted by Interpol and Scottish law enforcement. They turned out to be part of a group who had blackmailed more than one thousand victims, including Daniel. Three men who were among those arrested are believed specifically to have blackmailed Daniel.

Assistant Chief Constable Malcolm Graham noted,[10] "A young Scottish teenager lost his life as a result of this online activity. The impact on his family, friends, and wider community cannot be imagined. There is no hiding place—anywhere in the world."

The FBI posted on its website some cases it has been working on and a map showing locations of identified sextortion victims in the United States and Canada,[11] including this one:

Ashley Reynolds was a happy 14-year-old who loved sports, did well in school academically and socially, and enjoyed keeping a journal she intended her "future self" to read. But what happened in the summer of 2009 was so devastating that she couldn't bring herself to record it in her diary—or speak about it to anyone.

She had become the victim of sextortion, a growing Internet crime in which young girls and boys are often targeted. Her life was being turned upside down by an online predator who took advantage of her youth and vulnerability to terrorize her by demanding that she send him sexually explicit images of herself.

After several months, Ashley's parents discovered what was happening and contacted the National Center for Missing & Exploited Children (NCMEC). Ashley and her parents later supported the FBI investigation that led to the arrest of 26-year-old Lucas Michael Chansler, who last year pled guilty to multiple counts of child pornography production and was sent to prison for 105 years—but not before he used the Internet to victimize nearly 350 teenage girls. The majority of those youngsters have not yet been identified.

The FBI's website offers advice on how kids and teens can stay safer online and not become the victim of a sextortionist:

Whatever you are told online may not be true, which means the person you think you are talking to may not be the person you really are talking to. . . . Don't send pictures to strangers. Don't post any pictures of yourself online that you wouldn't show to your grandmother. If you only remember that, you are probably going to be safe.

Interpol also advises that anyone who believes he is being targeted should immediately cease all contact with the individual and report the matter to the local police and online service provider. If it is via a social network, the administrator should also be alerted, and talk to a trusted adult—do not try to keep it to yourself.

"Do not pay money that is being demanded," Interpol adds.[12] "You are not the only one to fall for these scams but you can help to stop them by reporting it as quickly as possible and by refusing to pay. If you are a child please talk to a trusted adult. It may seem there is no way out, but there are people who can help."

CHAPTER EIGHT

Social Media Websites and Apps

Do you remember when Myspace[1] was "the" place to be online? If you are a kid or teen, you probably don't even know what Myspace is. Trust me: that was the biggest social media website on the Internet at one time.

These days not only are there social media websites, but there are social media apps for smartphones, tablets, and other Internet-connected devices.

Although Facebook currently is the "king" of social media, kids and teens are just a bit too cyber savvy at times for their parents when it comes to social media.

Popular sites and apps kids and teens use besides Facebook include Twitter, Ask.fm, Instagram, Kik, Periscope, Vine, Snapchat, Whisper, Secret, ooVoo, and too many more to count.[2] The majority of them proclaim that they keep users anonymous, which makes them all the more troubling.

Colleen (pseudonym),[3] a fifteen-year-old from New York City, had been dating her boyfriend for a few months and was getting irked that one of his female friends had started flirting with him online. She told Mark (pseudonym)[4] that this made her uncomfortable and asked if he could block Jane (pseudonym)[5] on all of his social media accounts. He did in January 2015 to save their relationship, but somehow Jane realized Colleen had asked Mark to block her, even though he and Colleen had not been rude or mean to her.

"She and her friends began Snapchatting me videos, calling me a slut and saying they don't like me," Colleen said. "They posted all over their Twitter accounts how they were going to ruin my life and called me a slut, psycho bitch, hoe, etcetera. They called my boyfriend a loser, asshole, etcetera. They do this because they were jealous that he would rather have me as his girlfriend than them as friends."

One friend of Jane's friends threatened to confront Colleen offline and punch her. Colleen had told her mother about the posts, but not the possible physical confrontation because she didn't want to worry her. But Colleen did the right thing—not only did she tell an adult, but she showed her friends the bullying messages to let them know what was going on and did not respond to them in any way.

However, she did keep screenshots as evidence and began blocking Jane on all of her social media accounts. She then changed her settings so that only people on her friend and contact lists could post on any of her social media profiles. She also went through her contact lists and made sure she knew everyone on them.

For a tenth grader, Colleen was very tech savvy—and knowledgeable enough to know that defending herself or fighting back would be a bad idea. She got friend requests from some questionable accounts soon after and did not accept them, thinking they were Jane or her friends. She probably was right about that.

By the spring, the brouhaha calmed down, and the bullying and harassment stopped. If she had allowed anonymous messages to be sent to her or posted on her social media accounts, the bullying probably would have continued.

"My work with students indicates that anonymous apps tend to bring out the worst in people," Mike Dreiblatt, president of standuptobullying.net, said. "For some students, their middle school and high school years are a time of very strong emotions. Some students use anonymous apps to strike at someone virtually that they can't strike at in real life. Sometimes, teenagers lash out anonymously because they think the other person started it. Some cyberbullying is inadvertent. They think they've made a joke. They think it's funny, and friends egg them on. Later they can't believe what they said." He also feels it is taking too long for social media websites and apps to enact measures not only to better protect users, but to combat cyberbullying.[6]

An article by Sarah Lacy on Pando.com[7] caught Secret cofounder and CEO David Byttow by surprise. Titled "Now That We've Seen Secret's Ugly Soul, Will Investors Act?," the article pretty much skewered the Secret app as being "uncaring about cyberbullying."

This caused Byttow immediately to make changes in the app. If users typed in certain keywords or images, a notice would pop up to give them a chance to "rethink" what they want to post. And it would not allow some names or words to be posted at all.

The Whisper app decided to do something as well. It has a nonprofit website called Your Voice[8] where people can post stories in video format about things that have happened to them online that led them to depression, thoughts of suicide, and more. All of the videos are poignant and touching and offer others who are thinking of killing themselves a chance to rethink their actions. "Depression doesn't define you—you're so much more," "This life is so worth living," "Find those that build you up, not tear you down," and "Labels do not define your future" are just a few of the messages posted as an introduction to the posted videos.

On January 7, 2016, Reid Adler killed himself after a friend on Facebook threatened to post a compromising photo of Reid on social media. The fifteen-year-old, a freshman at Ralston High School in Omaha, was remembered as being happy-go-lucky and fun to be around. No one knew at first why he had killed himself. Only afterward did his parents discover he had been bullied on social media and through texts on his smartphone. This had been going on for months, but Reid did not confide in anyone about it.

"He had the biggest heart. He would do anything for anybody. He was always that guy who left no person out," said Mark Adler, Reid's father.[9]

As far as anyone knew, Reid was happy with his life. He was involved in football, basketball, and track at school, had friends over to his house often, and was always asking what fun things would be happening the next day. No one had a clue to his depression.

Students from his high school told people that students often bullied each other on temporary accounts set up on Instagram, Facebook, and Snapchat, then would delete the accounts afterward.

Just the idea that anyone can create an account, use it to bully and harass, then delete it so easily is hard to imagine. But it happens every day.

Experts call on social media websites and apps to do more to combat cyberbullying.

"At times it feels like it is taking too long, but anonymous apps are getting better at following commonsense policies and procedures that limit bullying and ensure kids' safety," noted Dreiblatt. "That said, anonymous apps still have a long way to go. Unfortunately, unless there is a long and sustained public outcry, I think investors and advertisers will participate in anonymous apps if they think it is financially advantageous."[10]

In February 2016, Facebook launched a suicide prevention tool in the United Kingdom.[11] In 2015 this same tool was released in the United States, then in Australia in December 2015, with other countries to follow. The tool, developed with the Samaritans, provides support for those who are contemplating suicide, their family, and friends. With more than six thousand recorded suicides in 2014 in the United Kingdom and more than half of the UK population on Facebook (estimated to be thirty-six million people), Facebook felt it needed to provide something to combat an ever-growing problem.

The tool works this way: If someone suspects a friend or family member is considering suicide or is depressed, he can flag the concerning post. A twenty-four-hour team at Facebook will review the flagged post and if the person is deemed suicidal, an anonymous post is sent to him with a simple message: "Hi, a friend thinks you might be going through something difficult and asked us to look at your recent post." Only that user can see this post, and anything done in response is private.

The user can see the post or click on "Continue." He is then directed to links to talk to someone online or via phone or get tips and support.

Twitter rolled out its own anti-bullying tools in 2015[12] offering support to its users and resources to use to stop the cyberbullying or harassment.

Richard Guerry, executive director of IROC2,[13] notes, "In my opinion, apps that market themselves as 'Anonymous' need to do a better job clearly informing their users that they are not really 'anonymous' and that individuals can be identified and reported to law enforcement in the event their account illustrates abuse of their platform for cruelty, harassment, or threats. Some platforms and apps like Ask.fm and Whisper do state that they do share information with law enforcement when necessary, however they hide this information in the privacy policy, which many users do not read."

Is it too little too late? Let's hope not.

How can online users prevent cyberbullying and harassment on their own accounts? Quite simply: change privacy and user settings. The majority of social media websites and apps let anyone who is on their site or using their app automatically see you when you sign up for an account. That's the default. They don't alert you to change your settings; you need to do it yourself if you know how.

Many social media users have no clue what to do when they are attacked anonymously online.

- First, refuse the bullying by responding with a very simple "Please stop contacting me."
- Next, report the bullying or harassment to the site or app. A default e-mail address to use would be abuse@sitename.com (or org, depending on their domain). Many websites and apps have buttons or links to report the abuse quickly. On others you need to hunt for it, but clicking

on "Privacy," "Support," or something similar should help. Then delete and block the user who is bullying or harassing from your friend, follower, or other list.

- Next, go into the privacy and user settings on your profile and select what you want. The default selection set up by the site or app usually is "public," or "worldwide," or something similar; change the setting to friends only (or followers, or whatever is the designation for users you are communicating with).
- Go through your friends or followers list and make sure you know them. If you don't, then delete them. You are not being rude—just protecting yourself and making your online profile safer.
- Change personal information in your profile that other users can see. Delete your cell or home phone numbers, home or work address, birth date or e-mail address; make sure other users can't view that information. If someone wants to contact you in a way other than on the social media site or app, she can send a direct message or private message and ask for that contact information.
- Finally, make sure posted photos or videos are something you wouldn't mind having disseminated elsewhere online. Anything sexually provocative, underage smoking or drinking, giving the finger, doing drugs or other illegal activities—these can and will get people into a whole heap of trouble and will follow them well into the future. Like sexting, they could cause you to get kicked out of school, lose a scholarship or opportunity to go to the college or university of your dreams, lose a job, ruin a relationship, cause problems in a court case, and much more.

If the cyberbullying or harassment continues after you have done everything to try to stop it, make sure to save everything—screen shots, e-mails, photos, texts, and so forth. If you receive death threats or threats of physical harm, immediately file a report with the police. Tell someone what is going on: don't keep it inside like Reid did and try to make it look like everything is hunky-dory.

It will take time to go through all the user and privacy settings on all of the social media accounts users have, but in the long run it will be worth it. Not only will they be safer online, they could be saving their own lives.

"If social media apps and sites clearly marketed a zero tolerance policy for abuse—as clearly and as strongly as they market the benefit of 'anonymity' (to generate downloads, reach and revenue)—I believe we would see a reduction of cruelty across these platforms," Richard Guerry added. "Unfortunately, there is no way to completely eliminate user abuse of social media and apps as it relates to cyber cruelty. However, I do believe some users would be less cavalier about the cruel things they post if they understand they aren't absolutely anonymous and could be caught."[14]

Parents (and other adults) also need to know some of the more common acronyms kids and teens use on social media websites and apps, such as the following:[15]

1. **OOTD**—Outfit of the day.
2. **KOTD**—Kicks of the day. Typically it refers to sneakers.
3. **HMU**—Hit me up. Usually it's asking for someone's Snapchat username, a phone number to text, or for a direct message.
4. **Smash**—I would have sex with you. A girl might post a provocative picture, and a boy might write "smash."
5. **Cook session**—That's when one or several teens gang up on another kid on social media.
6. **TBH**—To be honest. A teen might post a picture of himself and ask for a TBH, usually looking for positive responses.
7. **TBR**—To be rude. Although TBH often leads to positive responses, TBR usually is followed by a negative response.
8. **OOMF**—One of my followers. It's a secretive way to talk about one of their followers without saying their name, such as "OOMF was so hot today."
9. **BAE**—Baby. It's an affectionate term for someone's girlfriend or boyfriend.
10. **WCW**—Woman Crush Wednesday. A girl will post a picture of another girl she thinks is pretty, whereas guys will post pictures of girls they think are hot.
11. **MCM**—Man Crush Monday. It's similar to Woman Crush Wednesday, but it features pictures of men.
12. **BMS**—Broke my scale. It's a way to say you like the way someone looks.
13. **RDH**—Rate date hate. As in "rate me, would you date me, do you hate me?" A typical response might be "rate 10 date yes hate no" or "10/y/n."
14. **IDK**—I don't know.
15. **RN**—Right now.
16. **KIK**—Another social media app, Kik, to communicate on.
17. **FML**—F*** my life.

18. **AF**—As f***. A teen might tweet "mad af" or "you seem chill af."
19. **LMAO**—Laughing my ass off.
20. **S/O or SO**—Shout out.
21. **ILYSM**—I like you so much or I love you so much.
22. **CWD**—Comment when done. Similar to TBH, urging others to comment on the photo of whatever they're posting.
23. **LOL**—Laugh out loud. Yes, you'll still find teens using LOL and OMG.

Some of these acronyms will be familiar to many adults, but if you see something more like:

w@7ch 0u7 4 r3n7$ 0v3r $h0uld3r

then you have encountered Leetspeak. This is an elite language many kids and teens use because adults have caught onto OMG, LOL, and so forth. What kids and teens do is replace letters with numbers and symbols. For example:

- A = 4
- C = (
- E = 3
- F = Ph
- G = 9
- H = |-|
- I = 1
- K = |<
- M = /\/\
- N = |/|
- O = 0
- S = 5 (of $)
- T = 7
- W = \/\/
- X = ><
- Y = '/

So,

w@7ch 0u7 4 r3n7$ 0v3r $h0uld3r

would be in English:

Watch out for parents over shoulder

Here are some other examples—it's easy to catch on once you get the hang of it:

- Leetspeak = 13375p34k
- You are so cool = u 4r3 50 (001
- Who knows = \/\/h0 k||0\/\/5

Several converters online will convert from Leetspeak to English, or vice versa. Just type "Leetspeak converter" or "Leetspeak generator" in a search engine and choose the one you feel suits you. Then amaze your kids and teens by sending them a message in Leetspeak!

CHAPTER NINE

Cell and Smartphone Know-how

Sexting was covered in chapter 7, but what happens when a cell or smartphone is used to bully and harass?

Justina (pseudonym),[1] who lived in Maine, began to receive bullying texts about her sexual orientation in April of 2015 from three New York boys.

"They were assuming things about my friend and I, calling us offensive slurs, and making death threats to people of the same sexual orientation," recalled Justina.

It happened because she had dated one of the boys, Lenny (pseudonym),[2] for a few months but broke it off because she felt it wasn't working out as she had hoped. He texted her, trying to woo her back, but she wouldn't give in.

"I added my friend to the text conversation for support, and in response he added two of his friends," Justina said.

That was just the beginning of the bullying texts and messages.

Lenny and his friends would text her that they would do bad things to Justina and her friend, such as torturing, burning, and killing them. She and her friend were frightened that he and his friends would drive from Buffalo, New York, to where they lived in Maine, but they didn't report it to anyone.

"I blocked him on my cell phone and on Instagram and so far, he and the others haven't tried to contact me or my friend again," Justina said.

She learned a powerful lesson, though—don't include other friends on a message like she did, or things quickly could escalate out of control.

"If I could do it again, I would never have responded the way I did," Justina noted.

She was lucky it didn't turn into a physical confrontation.

On July 13, 2014, eighteen-year-old Conrad Roy III was found dead of carbon monoxide poisoning in his truck in a K-Mart parking lot in Massachusetts.

Surprisingly, the bully who put Conrad over the edge was his own girl-friend, Michelle Carter, also eighteen. Texts were used as evidence in her trial in August 2015.

"You have to just do it," Michelle texted him, according to court docu-ments.[3] "You have everything you need. There is no way you can fail. Tonight is the night. It's now or never."

The indication was that Conrad was having second thoughts, but she encouraged him to commit suicide.

"Everyone will be sad for a while but they will get over it and move on," she texted him. "You always say you're gonna do it, but you never do. I just want to make sure tonight is the real thing."

She did research online for him on how to kill himself and told him how to siphon the carbon monoxide into his truck.

"But I bet you're gonna be like 'oh, it didn't work because I didn't tape the tube right or something like that,'" she texted. "I bet you're gonna say an excuse like that . . . you seem to always have an excuse."

She also offered him other options to kill himself—putting a bag over his head or hanging himself.

On the day he killed himself, Conrad took his younger sisters out for an ice cream. He and Michelle exchanged texts while he was with his sisters.

Conrad: "I just don't know how to leave them, you know."

Michelle: "Say you're gonna go to the store or something."

Conrad: "Like, I want them to know that I love them."

Michelle: "They know. That's one thing they definitely know. You're overthinking."

Conrad: "I know I'm overthinking. I've been overthinking for a while now."

Michelle: "I know. You just have to do it like you said. Are you gonna do it now?"

In April 2015, Michelle was indicted on involuntary manslaughter charges.

"Instead of attempting to assist him or notify his family or school officials, Ms. Carter is alleged to have strongly influenced his decision to take his own life, encouraged him to commit suicide and guided him in his engagement of activities which led to his death," Gregg Miliote, director of communica-tions for the Bristol County District Attorney's Office, said in a statement.

Her defense attorney, Joseph Cotaldo, claimed in court that she was "brainwashed" by Conrad, although the text messages she sent to him appear to show otherwise.

Cotaldo attempted to have the involuntary manslaughter charges thrown out, but the case was continued in January 2016. It was referred to the Judicial Supreme Court, and Carter was banned from using Facebook or other social media while the case was ongoing. She faces up to twenty years in prison if found guilty. And the rest of her life has been ruined as a result of her senseless actions . . . and texts.

On July 2, 2016, it was ruled that Carter must stand trial for involuntary manslaughter.

"In sum, we conclude that there was probable cause to show that the coercive quality of the defendant's verbal conduct overwhelmed whatever willpower the eighteen year old victim had to cope with his depression, and that but for the defendant's admonishments, pressure, and instructions, the victim would not have gotten back into the truck and poisoned himself to death," Justice Robert Cordy wrote for the court in the unanimous ruling.[4]

Smartphones and cell phones are in just about everyone's hands, all over the world. Most use them responsibly, but some, as in the two examples, use these tools inappropriately without thinking about the consequences.

One man found out the hard way why it's not a good idea to keep nude photos on your smartphone. Philip Sherman of Bella Vista, Arkansas, visited a McDonald's for a quick bite to eat in Fayetteville on July 5, 2008. He left without his smartphone. Someone found it, discovered nude photos of his wife on it, and posted them online. They also texted his wife. And this happened *after* Philip had called the McDonald's and asked employees to keep the smartphone safe. Talk about being embarrassed.

Philip and his wife, Tina, sued McDonald's Corp. and the manager of the location where he left his smartphone. The lawsuit,[5] alleging McDonald's employees breached a duty to "protect and secure" the contents of his phone, sought $3 million in damages.

It took a few years, but on February 26, 2010, McDonald's Corp. and the franchisee settled the case. Although the settlement was not made public, all parties involved were pleased with the outcome.

"We are pleased that this matter has been concluded," Bill Mathews, coowner of the McDonald's franchise, said in a statement. "We strive to provide a safe and positive environment for all our customers. We respect their privacy."

Clearly, he should not have kept the nude photos on his smartphone, even though they were from his wife to him. But what should you do in the event that you are being harassed or bullied on your smartphone or cell phone? What else can you do to keep your smartphone or cell phone safe?

First, if you know the name and/or number the harassing or bullying texts are coming from, take a screen shot showing the text and number.

Second, tell your cell phone provider about the texts—the company may offer helpful advice.

Third, do an online search of the number that texted you. Put the phone number in quotes in the search engine box—such as "800-111-1234"—so the results you get are more refined. Go through the top results to determine what cell phone provider that number is associated with. Once you have that information, let the provider know that one of its users is harassing you.

Fourth, if the texts threaten physical harm or death, contact law enforcement—preferably in person so you can show the screen shots or actual texts and identify the cell phone provider the harasser or bully is using.

Finally, change the settings on your smartphone or cell phone. First block the number from being able to text you again. Your cell phone provider's website or the website of the type of phone you own should have instructions on how to do this. If in doubt, contact your cell phone provider's local store to see if someone can help you.

Kaspersky Lab[6] offers these tips on keeping your smartphone or cell phone safer:

- **Keep it locked.**

Keep your phone's screen lock on—at all times—so there's less at risk if your phone falls into the hands of a cybercriminal.

- **Monitor how apps behave on your phone.**

Be aware of permission access/requests from applications running on your phone. It's especially important to do this for Android smartphones.

- **Switch off Bluetooth . . . when you can.**

If you're not using your Bluetooth connection, switch it off. That way, you'll make your phone less vulnerable to cyberattack . . . and you'll reduce the drain on your phone's battery.

- **Choose a smartphone security solution with anti-theft features.**

Some smartphone security products include a range of anti-theft features that give you remote access to your lost or stolen phone—so you can lock the phone, wipe data from it, and find its location.

Another good resource is the Identity Theft Resource Center,[7] which offers a lot of information on keeping your smartphone or cell phone safe, including:

- Be aware of what you are doing on your phone. The same precautions you would take while on your home computer apply to your smartphone. Double-check URLs for accuracy, don't open suspicious links, and make sure a site is secure (https) before giving any billing or personal information.
- When installing an app on any smartphone, take the time to read the "small print." Evaluate the information the app requires access to, and consider whether it is necessary for the app to run successfully. If you cannot see a reason for the app to have access to the information, you should reconsider installing it.
- Limit your activities while using public Wi-Fi. Try not to make purchases or access e-mail while using a public Wi-Fi zone. Hackers target public Wi-Fi hotspots because the hacker gets direct access to your mobile device. Use your 3G or 4G network provider connection—it is much more secure than a public Wi-Fi connection.

One wonders if Philip Sherman had known all of the above, would those photos have ended up online after all?

CHAPTER TEN

When Online Fun and Gaming Goes Wrong

Before there was Gamergate,[1] there was swatting.[2] This is when someone calls 911 and files a false report that some sort of incident is in progress at a certain address. The reports range from a home invasion, to kidnapping, to a potential homicide/suicide situation, terrorist threat, bomb threat, to just about anything that would warrant an emergency response. The larger the response, the bigger the mental "reward" for the caller. The caller gets bonus points if a SWAT team or bomb squad shows up, even more if police helicopters or the National Guard show up.

In February 2016, an Internet meme appeared online of a Riverside, California, teenager named Josh Holz repeating "Damn, Daniel" for thirty seconds as he videotaped his friend, Daniel Lara, walking around in his white Vans sneakers. It was retweeted more than 290,000 times on Twitter and was featured on entertainment news shows.

But someone didn't like how popular it made Daniel.

Riverside police got a phone call at around 1 a.m. on February 23, 2016. The caller claimed that Daniel had killed his mother with an AK-47. The response was swift. Luckily, there was no murder. After going through the recording of the 911 call, it was determined that a vocal modulation device was used to hide the caller's real voice.

"We believe and the family believes that since their video went viral, it's somehow connected," said Riverside police lieutenant Kevin Townsend.[3] "Ever since their video has gone out there, they've received a number of what they call strange phone calls and e-mails, and a lot of strange things happening so tonight was just another incident for their family."

Ultimately, Josh removed the "Damn, Daniel" video from Twitter, causing many to think "Damn, Josh." But you can still see the video by searching online for "Damn, Daniel."

When twenty-year-old Tyran Cobbs of Ellicott City, Maryland, was swatted, the results weren't quite as tame. He was hit in the face with rubber bullets the police shot.

The Howard County Police claimed that someone saying he was Cobbs called 911 in July 2015 and said he was going to execute three hostages if he didn't received $15,000 by a certain deadline.

Police arrived and saw Cobbs in the apartment with three women. They contacted Cobbs's father, whose name was on the apartment lease. He said he honestly didn't know whether the threat was credible. So the police were pretty suspicious, even when one of the women came to the door and said there was no emergency. Even stranger, Cobbs crawled on the floor in front of sliding glass doors twice, was ordered to stand up and show his hands but did not. That's when police shot two nonlethal rubber bullets at him.

Once he was sent to the hospital, police searched the apartment and determined there had indeed been no threat. Police never tracked down who made the false 911 call, the fourth one involving swatting to date that year.

In this case, the swatting involved online gaming. Someone who had been playing the online game with him was upset that Cobbs was beating him and made the swatting call as revenge.

The FBI warned of swatting as far back as 2008,[4] and it has arrested numerous people since then; some currently are in federal prison as a result.

"The FBI looks at these crimes as a public safety issue," said Kevin Kolbye, an assistant special agent in charge in the Dallas division of the FBI. "It's only a matter of time before somebody gets seriously injured as a result of one of these incidents."

The cost of emergency response to swatting incidents is in the thousands of dollars, even more so if specialized units, such as a SWAT team, are called in.

"The victims are scared and taken by surprise," Kolbye said. "They (law enforcement) believe they have a violent subject to apprehend or an innocent victim to rescue. It's a dangerous situation any way you look at it."

One case highlighted on the FBI website is known as the Matthew Weigman Case:[5]

In 2009, Matthew Weigman, then 19 years old, was sentenced to more than 11 years in federal prison for a swatting conspiracy that had been going on for years.

A prolific phone hacker, Weigman and nine co-conspirators used social engineering and other scams to obtain personal information, impersonate and harass telecommunications employees, and manipulate phone systems to carry out dozens of swatting incidents, along with other crimes. Several of his co-conspirators also received jail time.

Weigman's first swatting incident occurred in 2004 when he was 14 years old. When a girl he met through an online chat room refused to have phone sex with him, he retaliated by swatting the girl and her father, convincing a 911 operator he was holding the two at gunpoint in their Colorado home, which prompted a SWAT response.

Even more terrifying, because he lost playing an online game, a teenager can end up in jail for pretty much the rest of his life, or he might as well be.

That's what happened to Paul Homer, who was fifteen years old in 2014 when he was convicted on felony charges of swatting. He broke down in tears in the courtroom when he was told he would serve twenty-five years to life in federal prison because after he lost an online game he made a false 911 call.

Going by the gamer screen name of BadAssDwg69, he was repeatedly beaten by a fellow gamer while playing Battlefield 4,[6] a first-person shooter game. He engaged the winner online, finding out personal information, then searched online for more information. Once he had a home address for his opponent, he called in a murder/hostage situation to 911. A SWAT team was dispatched. They raided the house, then shot and critically injured the father who answered the door.

Once the phone call was traced to Homer, the 2011 Patriot Act was used to charge him as an adult because of the seriousness of the crime—two counts of domestic terrorism related to his manipulation of an enforcement response and injuries to innocents resulting from those actions.

It didn't help when prosecutors played the 911 call for jurors.

"I just shot and killed four people. If any police enter my home, I will kill them too," said the caller (Homer).[7]

Prosecuting attorney Jack Phillips claimed, "Horner's actions are pure evil; he is a menace to society and must be prosecuted to the fullest extent of the law."

Court proceedings revealed Homer's online persona as brave, brash, and a bit cocky. In real life, he broke down in tears several times in court, once sobbing so hysterically the judge had to remove him from the courtroom.

After pronouncing the sentence, Judge Arthur Digsby told Homer that although he felt bad for Homer, he was still responsible for what he did.

"Ignorance of consequence because of lack of thought absolves no one," the judge said. "Thinking that your actions were only a prank did not make them only a prank."

Before banging his gavel and ending the session, the judge had this advice for anyone who thought swatting was a good thing: "Leave your petty pride in the realm of digital fantasy where it is still safe," Digsby said. "Because, as young mister Horner has learned, actions in the real world don't have a reset button. And every parent should make sure their children understand that."

The FBI site notes that some swatters are pretty sophisticated when it comes to getting your information to make a false 911 call. One case[8] in Dallas was particularly intriguing:

Five swatters in several states targeted people who were using online telephone party chat lines (or their family or friends). The swatters found the victims' personal details by accessing telecommunication company information stored on protected computers. Then, by manipulating computer and phone equipment, they called 911 operators around the country. Using "spoofing technology," the swatters made it appear the calls were coming from the victims.

Between 2002 and 2006, the five swatters called 911 lines in more than sixty cities nationwide, impacting more than one hundred victims, disrupting services for telecommunications providers and emergency responders, and resulting in up to $250,000 in losses.

The group's "swats" included using bomb threats at sporting events, causing the events to be delayed; claiming that hotel visitors were armed and dangerous, causing the entire hotel to be evacuated; and making threats against public parks and officials.

The swatters were tracked down through the cooperative efforts of local, state, and federal agencies and the assistance of telecommunications providers and first responders. In all, the case involved more than forty state and local jurisdictions in about a dozen states. All five subjects pled guilty to various charges and were sentenced in 2008.

Why did they do it? According to Kevin Kolbye, assistant special agent in charge of the Dallas FBI office, "Individuals did it for the bragging rights and ego, versus any monetary gain."

Basically, they did it because they could.

Swatting doesn't happen only in the United States. Identified only as "BLA" (due to privacy laws in Canada), a seventeen-year-old in Vancouver thought he had a unique way to get back at females who refused his friend requests, chats, and obscene messages. He targeted others in the online game League of Legends. His list of "enemies" seemed endless.

He made false 911 calls to their homes, bringing in SWAT teams; hacked their computers; and posted their personal information online for the world to see. He targeted females all over North America, in Canada and the United States, causing a school to shut down and Disneyland to close part of its entertainment complex. He called in a fake hostage situation to a house in January 2014, then further terrorized that family by circulating their financial data online and allowing others to steal the family's identities.

Arrested in March of 2014 and released on bail, BLA was arrested again that October. He couldn't stop his apparent obsession with harming others online. He remained in jail until his sentencing.

BLA received a sixteen-month prison sentence after he pleaded guilty to twenty-three charges, including extortion, harassment, and public mischief. Because of time served, he was released, but he spent another eight months being supervised in the community and was banned from using the Internet while serving his sentence.

His excuse?

"I had a lot of time on my hands," he said. "I don't do anything productive, and that leaves me time to do criminal activity."[9]

The United Kingdom has swatters who apparently like to bother people in the United States.

Going by the online persona Ransom (privacy laws in England prevent publishing an underage person's name), a sixteen-year-old boy from Bidston, England (near Liverpool), was arrested in June 2015 for swatting incidents against airlines and police departments from October 29, 2014, to March 26, 2015, using Skype, Twitter, MSN Messenger, and e-mail. In addition, from September 4, 2014, through April 20, 2015, Ransom allegedly made bomb threats on Twitter regarding Michigan universities, airlines, and airports, causing shutdowns and flight cancellations.

Police confiscated several computers and cell phones when they searched the teen's home. The case is ongoing.

In Australia, Queensland police were called to a home in June 2014 via a text message that a teen had killed his mother and was holding his father hostage.

Twenty police officers in bulletproof vests surrounded this house; the teen surrendered and was arrested. But when police searched the house, they could not find any evidence to support the text that was sent, allegedly from the teen's cell phone.

Matt McGrath, eighteen, had become Australia's first known swatting victim.

Police superintendent David Donohue voiced his frustration.

"It's not only frustrating but it's dangerous, it's dangerous to the police responding to the people inside the house," he told reporters.[10] "It will probably take weeks to months before we can find out through IP, servers, and back-tracking the electronic footprint."

McGrath was equally frustrated, claiming that his visit to a website called HackForums[11] (a grayhat hacking website) the night before possibly caused the incident. He said he fell asleep without logging off of the site and thinks someone there did the swatting.

Police confiscated three computers and one cell phone, although McGrath denied he sent the text, noting no such text was on his cell phone.

Swatting has gotten so bad that a federal law[12] is being considered to make swatting officially a federal crime. U.S. Reps. Patrick Meehan, Republican, of Pennsylvania, and Katherine Clark, Democrat, of Massachusetts, introduced the Interstate Swatting Hoax Act of 2015 in November. This law would make swatting a federal crime and hold perpetrators responsible for deaths or serious injuries that result from raids and for any associated costs.

Meehan noted at a press conference that hoax swatting calls are made more than four hundred times every year throughout the United States. Meehan described the essence of the bill: when a false report is intentionally designed to bring a SWAT response, the perpetrator could be prosecuted federally.

Although California and New Jersey have passed their own anti-swatting laws, a federal law would help, especially if the caller is in a different state from the victim.

Unfortunately, Clark got a taste of swatting on January 31, 2016. While at her Melrose, Massachusetts, home watching TV with her husband, blue lights suddenly shone in their windows. Looking outside, she was surprised to see police cruisers at either end of her street, blocking the road. Then she saw police officers with guns on her lawn.

"It's a pretty terrifying sight at 10 o'clock, after a nice weekend with your family," she said.[13]

When she opened the door, the police officers told her they were responding to a 911 call saying an active shooter was at her home. Playback of that call revealed the caller apparently had used a voice-altering device.

Clark deduced that the call was a result of her support for the anti-swatting. She was just relieved that only the local police, and not them plus a SWAT team, had come to her house. She tweeted the next day: "I'm thankful no one was hurt & grateful for timeliness and professionalism of #Melrose Police Dept."

The incident didn't scare Clark: she has no intentions of backing down and is now even more determined to see the anti-swatting bill pass. "If that was the intent of calling in this event," Clark said, "I think they have underestimated my commitment to making sure that we do stop this practice."

Controlling Privacy Settings on Video Game Systems

Nintendo Wii U—http://en-americas-support.nintendo.com/app/answers/landing/p/431/c/188

Nintendo Wii—http://en-americas-support.nintendo.com/app/answers/landing/p/604/c/628

Nintendo 3DS—http://en-americas-support.nintendo.com/app/answers/landing/p/430/c/184

Nintendo DSi—http://en-americas-support.nintendo.com/app/answers/landing/p/696/c/184

Nintendo General Information for Parents (includes Netflix parental controls, how to block the Internet, and more)—http://www.nintendo.com/consumer/into/_na/parents.jspPlaystation 4 (PS4); https://support.us.playstation.com/articles/en_US/KC_Article/PS4-Parental-Controls/?

Playstation 3 (PS3); http://www.nintendo.com/consumer/info/en_na/parents.jsp

Playstation 4 (PS4)—https://support.us.playstation.com/articles/en_US/KC_Article/PS4-Parental-Controls/?

Playstation 3 (PS3) and PSP—http://www.cnet.com/news/protect-your-children-how-to-set-parental-controls-on-the-ps3-psp/

Playstation Vita—http://manuals.playstation.net/document/en/psvita/basic/kids.html

Xbox 360—http://support-origin.xbox.com/en-US/xbox-360/security/xbox-live-parental-control

CHAPTER ELEVEN

When an Adult Is a Cyberbully

In January 2015, Joanna Tierno[1] got a message from a fellow eBay member interested in an item Joanna had put up for auction on eBay. It was a vintage collectible doll in its original box.

Dear joanna,
   Hi I usually don't offer because I didn't realize it takes 2 days to get an answer to my offer. I'm trying to get this doll to give to my Mother for a gift for Valentine's Day when I go back home to visit her. The doll has an eery resemblance to a drawing of a girl my Mother used to do for me when I was a wee young'in. There's also another doll of this same one finishing in four hours yet today. Please if you see my message for offer let me know right away and thank you.
                                                                              —Sarah[2]

Dear Sarah,
   I always answer right away. What is your offer?
                                                                              —Joanna

Dear joanna,
   Thank you for accepting my offer. My Mother will be over the moon. I have looked hard today to find the drawings today that she made me and I know I kept them. She used to love drawing the little girl and giving pictures of her to me for a thrill I guess. Sometimes she would put a bow in her hair just like this doll. But, it was the face that caught my attention and the hair do. Thanks again.
                                                                              —Sarah

Dear Sarah,
   That is so awesome! I am glad she will be enjoyed.
                                                                              —Joanna

Joanna Tierno. © Joanna Tierno.

Once Sarah paid through Paypal, Joanna carefully packaged the doll and shipped it to the address provided. She got a friend request on Facebook from the buyer and happily accepted it. A few days later, the package was returned to Joanna. Confused, she contacted Sarah.

Dear Sarah,
    Your package was returned to me today. UPS says you refused it. Shipping was nearly $20 & they will charge for redelivery, though I can try USPS next time. Let me know what you want to do.

—Joanna

The doll Joanna Tierno sent to the buyer. © Joanna Tierno.

Dear joanna,

Well Seller, when you send a box that is suppose [sic] to have a fragile collector doll in it and that box is rattling with movement in it galore of course it was refused by me. The UPS driver rang my door bell and put the box on my front door mate [sic]. I opened the door, pick up the box and it was noisy, movement in the box (rattling galore). I called to the driver, refused the box and it was sent back to you. Obviously you have it so refund my money please, so what's the issue? All else falls into place as you know once you do the right thing by me and refund my money to my account. No claims get filed with PayPal, my credit card or UPS, that is now aware of why it was refused! Expect to see refund today. Then we can be in touch again to finish process and no negative feedback will even be left. Be like we never met or had this transaction!

—Sarah

Dear Sarah,

Your doll is perfectly safe in a box in a box. She is not breakable. I assure you she is 100% in perfect condition.

—Joanna

The candy that was returned to Joanna in the doll box. © Joanna Tierno.

Joanna,

This box was sent back and as stated many times a refund is now due. Besides I have to get going today I have many calls to make. One is to a nice church called Oasis, among many other calls I will need to make today. I'm terribly busy to keep dealing with you and this box you sent that came rattling. Don't want it, is that clear enough for you! So let's just say a refund in 10 minutes (that would be 1:30 EST) or I can't wait online any more to see it and I have to get busy making those phone calls.

—Sarah

Totally confused, Joanna opened the package to find that the doll was no longer in the box and it had been replaced with a bag of mini Tootsie rolls. The mention of the church also bothered her. Why would the buyer call this church? She reached out to the pastor there and got her answer.

"This individual did call the church," the pastor told her. "I called her back. Evidently because of the blood drive we did here, she was under the impression you were a member of Oasis. She is a middle-aged woman who was rather upset about the whole situation with the eBay purchase. She felt the product was damaged."

Horrified, Joanna realized that Sarah had searched online and found out Joanna was involved in a blood drive recently held at the church. Joanna was born with hypogammaglobulinemia, a primary immune deficiency disease (PIDD). Treatment of her immune deficiency involved antibody replacement therapy, which is made possible by plasma (blood) donors. Joanna's involvement in the blood drive included being used in public service announcements and events as a spokesperson for PIDD.

She soon found out that Sarah had also called the New York Blood Center, then messaged members of Joanna's families and friends on Facebook about the eBay transaction, making it look like Joanna was the bad person. For example, she messaged Joanna's brother, Frank:

Hi Frank, you're related to Joanna Tierno. She sells on Ebay and I recognize her photo as being the same one shown on Ebay as shown on her Facebook page. Doing what I'm doing is totally uncomfortable by emailing relatives she knows. But, when I'm robbed on Ebay I certainly go after people who steal from me. I have tried to email her to no avail, her husband Chris and her son's girl-friend (who is actually who I first ended up finding) and emailing. Frank you and I are about the same age, I'm probably a tad younger then your Mother Anna. But, I believe you're related to Joanna as a sister-in-law. Joanna sent me a box through Ebay and she knows what she put in the box. This box has been sent back to her for a full refund through UPS. She should have it Monday Jan 19th. I'm writing to you today because of something Joanna posted on her Facebook page. Showing a cat watching a boxing match and the wording is hitting with your left and right etc. It's clearly a message to me. Because obviously I have asked her nicely now to do the right thing and refund my money for what's in the box (she knows what she did). This isn't easy doing these things and I certainly don't enjoy being put in this position to even have to try and get my own funds back. But, I need you to know and Joanna that I believe in the Lord with all that I am. I also can't explain this long detailed story but believe me when I say. I'm thinking God played a hand in us both having this transaction together on Ebay. I'm more then certain it's about both her and I learning a lesson. How to trust people and how we both must behave in life to even like ourselves. The irony is this isn't about the large sum of money she has now taken from me and won't refund. This is about human decency and I have to know this still exists in people or I fear I have lost all hope forever in forgiving not only Joanna but, every sole [sic] who has taken money from me on Ebay or any other aspect in my life. I'm saying I have been praying with all that I am that Joanna can and will do right by me. So with that restored Faith she gives me, I can do right by her (and she'll know what this means when she gets her own box back). But, this goes way beyond what Joanna did by stealing from me. It goes to having Faith in my fellow human beings to care, trust and treat each other with kindness and respect. This item I bought was to remind me of my Mom, who is 88 and dying right now. She can't even make it out of bed at the nursing home and has had a heart attack in November. So why and how Joanna could have done this to me when she knew with an email through Ebay why I bought her item is so evil, beyond evil. I have had sleepless nights since. Because when I knew a funeral would be coming up for my Mom soon enough and worrying over that. I knew I would see my own siblings at the funeral. I would have to find forgiveness finally after many years upon my Father's passing to forgive them from stealing with a so called "Lost Will" my Father had and finally I was ready to forgive. I'm saying so many people have dumped on me that with Joanna having done this now. I feel dead, morbid and alone. Like I can't trust any one, any more, any where in my whole life. I have people steal from me on Ebay, my own siblings steal from me with a so called lost Will and a husband who travels non-stop. I never see him anymore and don't feel we even connect.

What I bought from Joanna on Ebay was a resemblance of a much happier time in my life and reminded me of something very sweet my Mother once made for me and I told Joanna this. Why Joanna could or would do this to me is a mystery. I'm a total stranger and why she stole from me is beyond me but, all I did was buy an item from her and give her a sale. She took $105.00 from me and please talk with her and tell her I would like my money back when the box arrives tomorrow (Monday 19th) and I will do right by her too and forgive her. I don't need more hate in my heart, ever again. Thank you Frank

Joanna called UPS and discovered that the doll reached the buyer via UPS at 5:45 p.m. on January 15. The buyer returned the package on January 15 at 6:32 p.m. by taking it to a UPS driver/center, giving her enough time to replace the doll with the candy.

Joanna promptly reported and blocked Sarah on Facebook, then sent Sarah a message via eBay.

Dear Sarah,
I saw what you did. Return the doll to me & I will refund you your purchase

price minus shipping. No doll, no refund. Stealing isn't a nice way to live your life & its not like this is an item you need to survive. You should be very ashamed of yourself and should feel bad trying to steal from an individual like this. We all die one day & we don't bring our stuff with us. All that matters is the how you lived your life. Think carefully about what you do next—for yourself. When you are a bad person you diminish your own life. Is all you aim to be is a thief? And a liar? Do better by yourself and be a person you can be proud of.

—Joanna

Dear joanna,

What the world are you trying to pull lady! You had better have a way to explain this to the UPS, PayPal and Ebay. This package was refused and times logged for refusal, unless I'm having an affair with a UPS man. you had better have an explaination for all of this. This is going to my credit card today! They can deal with it and PayPal.

I also like I said before have way too many things to get done today to deal with a bad human like you on Ebay.

Nice try but now you have really made me a mad buyer

—Sarah

Dear Sarah,

You have to live with yourself. Return the doll & you will get a refund. Or if you want your box—just send shipping for the box.

—Joanna

Joanna was still trying to be civil about this, but the buyer was refusing to back down. The messages didn't stop coming. Dozens and dozens were being sent to Joanna, with implied threats, calling Joanna all sorts of names.

Now it was becoming cyberbullying.

Joanna reported Sarah to eBay several times, but nothing was done. Sarah received money from Joanna's Paypal account as a "refund," but when Joanna contacted Paypal and sent them some of the more harassing messages about the situation, they not only refunded the money to Joanna, but also canceled her Paypal credit card and issued a new one.

Joanna called the local police, who took a report and copies of the messages being sent to Joanna. Unless Joanna received a direct threat of physical harm or death, the police said they couldn't do very much because the buyer lived in Ohio and Joanna in New York. What were the chances of this woman coming to New York? To the police, very little.

Frustrated, Joanna turned to WHO@ for help. They showed her how to file a complaint again with eBay, then how to block Sarah on eBay from being able to see or bid on any of Joanna's further items. They then advised her to stop responding to Sarah but to keep anything that was sent to her. For Joanna, it was hard not to defend herself, but she did as WHO@ advised.

Joanna also posted on eBay's Community Sellers message board about the incident. Although most were sympathetic to her plight, several taunted her, frustrating her even more.

After searching on Sarah's eBay feedback profile, other sellers were found who had negative feedback from the same buyer. Joanna contacted them, and one wrote back to her:

> Joanna, Had a horrible experience with her back in 2006. Purchased multiple Bearingtons from me and complained about all of them and never returned them and ebay refunded all her money and she got all the bears. How did she get information about your family and friends and blood bank. I reported her to ebay as well and am very surprised that she is still on ebay

Although Joanna felt better knowing she wasn't the only seller who had been defrauded by this buyer, the bullying continued. When Sarah couldn't reach Joanna via eBay's messaging system, she soon began e-mailing Joanna directly.

What follows was the longest message, and almost enough of a threat to involve the police more, but they just added it to her case file:

> Dear joanna,
>
> Oh and the Facebook stuff. Lady you brought that public not me! I only emailed you privately to get my dough back! I told you a box would be arriving back to you soon. That it was rattling bad for a doll and I didn't want it. I told you once you open your own box we will talk. All will go full circle. I would have back what I started with (my own funds) and you would get back what you started with. But, your ugly rotten butt didn't do the right thing yet again! Instead you posted pictures publicly about what I sent back in your freaking doll box. Yes, I even told you I wanna you to open that box and know that feeling of what a buyer goes through when sellers pulled this shit of sending broken crap from Ebay. It's wrong, plain & simple, change your ways girl. Perhaps then you'll see more blessing come your way. I pray all the time and it does help. Even with the crappy body I was born with. But, I also pray for others suffering far worse in the world then my health issues. What kills me is you act and show yourself all over the Internet as some righteous, morale human being and you aren't. You have the negatives on here lady not me! I'm sure you've done it to others and some ladies just get scared to complain, Obviously I'm not one of them. You post a sign on your Facebook page gearing again to me, saying how just because your sick others think they can take

advantage of such a weakness. Lady your so full of bull and yourself U stink! So at least take that husband of yours out to eat on my money because even he didn't give a flying F-ing hoot if you robbed me you B!. When your both eating out, please by all means choke on the dinner & fall over dead! My message of course. But, I'd love to say God played a hand in me actually saying that. Your a mean, rotten thing of a human being for sending me this broken piece of crap doll! You needed this box of JUNK sent to your ugly butt (trying not to swear with my rotten crooks on Ebay). It's time us victims weed out the bad apples on Ebay. Ebay likes to stay neutral and frankly I can't blame them now. There are so many of you crooks using Ebay now. I don't even know how Ebay and PayPal keep up with all of you. Point is many regular users are aware that once our money goes out the door, it's now a toss up as to whether we'll get a good item anymore in using Ebay. My point: people like U running rampant on here now thinking they can just steal and hurt another human being. Not on my watch! Don't yeah get it many of you rotten users, keep doing these things we'll have less users bidding on our items. Oh I'm going to enclose pictures now of the JUNK CRAP CRACKED UP ROTTEN PIECE OF SHIT DOLL YOUR LYING BUTT SENT ME! Mattter of fact the pkg was rattling bad and movement galore in it when the UPS driver came up to the porch and rang the door bell. Thing is he was even concerned. Because when I opened the door, right that minute, I was right there getting my coat on at a closet ready to leave my house. I opened the door and heard all kinds of rattling as if the item wasn't even secure. I called the driver and told him listen I think the item in this pkg isn't what I bought (I bought a rather medium size doll that should be secure in a collector box and it shouldn't be rattling galore). He asked me if I wanted to check it, which I did think was nice. I did check it and we both saw how your box was mushed but the doll was broke! The driver said I'll take it back as it was already late into the evening and my UPS station is far from my home.

—Sarah

When Joanna didn't respond, just as WHO@ had advised, another message came from Sarah. She actually admitted to the candy.

YOU KNOW WHY THE DOLL CAME DAMAGED YOU B! YOU SENT IT DAMAGED u b! BUT, NOW, NOW I GO TO TOWN. WAIT AND SEE GIRL! ALSO EBAY GONNA BAD MOUTH YOU FROM NOW ON TOO BECAUSE YOU ALLOW THESE THINGS OF PEOPLE ROBBING FROM OTHERS SHAME ON YOU YOUR AS BAD AS THIS CROOK JOANNA! YES, YOU GOT CANDY b AND YOU'RE GOING TO GET A LOT MORE WHERE THAT CAME FROM! JUST WATCH. Ebay does't own the whole entire Internet! do they Ebay!!!!!!!!!!!!!!!!. I will tell my credit card about the f-ing CANDY too and why it was done because I have had nothing but lying crooks stealing my funds on Ebay for what seems like forever on this crap website!. By the way enjoy my candy you B! !@!!@!!! That's me cursing at your lying stealing butt and sending me broken crap, all my F-ing rotten crook sellers on here through the years. You too Ebay you protect all sellers at all costs and it stinks. Joanna I don't care anymore they can close it down. But, if it's the last thing I do in life I will make your life miserable you B! Like you've done to mine and cost you money, like you have with me!

WHO@ showed Joanna how to file a proper complaint with Sarah's Internet service provider about the e-mails. The messages stopped.

Finally, eBay removed the negative feedback Sarah had left on Joanna's profile.

And the doll? Presumably Sarah still has it.

Joanna learned one thing—if a package is returned, open it immediately to make sure it is the same item that was sent to the buyer, then file complaints through eBay and Paypal before engaging in any messages with the buyer, or she could be cyberbullied again.

This is just one example of how a complete stranger online can turn the tables on you—even an innocent eBay transaction can go wrong. Then there are those who are or were your friend, employer, significant other, online friend, and more.

It comes down to this: Try to not respond. Don't get involved in an online argument. Take a deep breath, and, if need be, unfriend and block the person. Your life will be better for it.

CHAPTER TWELVE

What Parents and Educators Need to Know

First, we will start with educators. Students may mention in passing that they were "dissed" or snubbed on Facebook or other social media or that they were taunted when they were playing an online video game. Although these incidents may have happened at home, but it won't be long before they will spill into their school life.

The Cyberbullying Research Center offers examples of cyberbullying scenarios[1] and what you, as an educator, can do to help the student in question. Here is one example:[2]

> James is frustrated and saddened by the comments his high school peers are making about his sexuality. Furthermore, it appears a group of male students has created an imposter account to impersonate him on an online dating site. Posing as James and using his contact information, they start sending out very provocative and sexually bold messages to other guys on the site. When James starts receiving e-mails from members of this site in his inbox, he is mortified and devastated.

If you were a school guidance counselor or administrator within the school, what would you do if James approached you with the problem?

Listening is the key in this situation. Don't interrupt while James is telling you what is happening. Once he has finished telling you about the situation, ask any questions you feel are necessary: does he know the names of the students who created the fake account in his name, where is that profile located, and has he filed a report about the fake profile with the online dating site? If he has not done that, you could help him navigate the website to file a proper complaint. Let James know that he is not at fault and you will do what you can to help him. Ask him if he has told his parents or guardians. If not, why not? He may be too embarrassed to do so. This could get touchy, but you may want to ask him if the two of you could meet with his parents or guardians to let them know what is happening and how you are helping him. It's better to do that now than later, when they may find out on their own and be upset that you had not contacted them. When and if you contact James's parents or guardians, emphasize that he had nothing to do with the fake profile, that he is embarrassed about the whole thing, and that he needs empathy at this time.

The parents or guardians most likely will want to know the students involved and may want to take action. If James knows the names of the students, then you and his parents can sit down with the principal to alert her to the situation and discuss what can be done about the students who created the fake profile.

There is no set way how to handle this type of situation, but you, as an educator, need to think about how you would handle it if it comes up at your school.

What happens when a situation becomes more involved, possibly violent? Here is a second example:

> Two female sixth graders, Katie and Sarah, are exchanging malicious texts because of a misunderstanding involving a boy named Jacob. The statements escalate in viciousness from trivial name-calling to very vicious and inflammatory statements, including death threats. Both girls have come to speak to the school counselor in tears, both angry at what is going on, and emotionally wrecked about the things being said online—that so many other students in their classes are seeing. In fact, other girls at school are getting involved and starting to take sides, leading to additional drama and even some minor physical violence at school.

The first question would be whether to involve the police. If your school has a school resource officer, it would be best to consult him. It appears that no crime has been committed, but maybe the resource officer can help cool things down.

The girls need to realize that threatening each other is not the answer, online or offline. First, they need to stop posting online and think about the situation. Is fighting over Jacob worth getting suspended from school? Is he worth hurting another person? Once they begin to think about the consequences of their actions, they may realize that things got out of control. They need to be reminded that what they post online is there forever. Would they want their parents, family members, or other people they know to see what they were posting about each other? Most likely the answer is "no."

Should the parents of both girls be contacted? Possibly and probably. Sit down with each girl and her parents and discuss the situation, then have a group meeting so that the girls can apologize to each other in person.

This is the preferred scenario, but each situation will be different. Be ready with questions to get at the root of the problem in order to defuse it.

The Cyberbullying Research Center offers a lot of resources for educators,[3] including a sample incident tracking form, games for students about cyberbullying, and a very helpful nine-page summary[4] that includes how to spot cyberbullying, how to respond to it, and how to try to prevent it from happening.

Top Ten Tips for Educators[5]

1. Formally assess the extent and scope of the problem within your school district by collecting survey and/or interview data from your students. Once you have a baseline measure of what is going on in your school, implement specific strategies to educate students and staff about online safety and Internet use in creative and powerful ways.

2. Teach students that all forms of bullying are unacceptable, and that cyberbullying behaviors are potentially subject to discipline. Have a conversation with students about what "substantial disruption" means. They need to know that even a behavior that occurs miles away from the school could be subject to school sanction if it substantially disrupts the school environment.

3. Specify clear rules regarding the use of the Internet, computers, and other electronic devices. Acceptable use policies tend to be commonplace in school districts, but these must be updated to cover online harassment. Post signs in school computer labs, hallways, and classrooms to remind students to use technology responsibly.

4. Use peer mentoring—where older students informally teach lessons and share learning experiences with younger students—to promote positive online interactions.

5. Consult with your school attorney *before* incidents occur to find out what actions you can or must take in varying situations.

6. Create a comprehensive formal contract specific to cyberbullying in the school's policy manual, or introduce clauses within the formal "honor code" that identify cyberbullying as inappropriate behavior.

7. Implement blocking/filtering software on your computer network to

prevent access to certain websites and software. Remember, a tech-savvy student can often find ways around these programs.

8. Cultivate a positive school climate; research has shown a link between a perceived "negative" environment on campus and an increased prevalence of cyberbullying offending and victimization among students. In general, it is crucial to establish and maintain a school climate of respect and integrity where violations result in informal or formal sanction.

9. Educate your community. Use a cyberbullying curriculum or general information sessions, such as assemblies and in-class discussions to raise awareness among youth. Invite specialists to talk to staff and students. Send information to parents. Sponsor a community education event. Invite parents, grandparents, aunts, uncles, and other relevant adults. Bribe them if necessary.

10. Designate a "cyberbullying expert" at your school who is responsible for educating himself or herself about the issues, then passing on important points to other youth-serving adults on campus.

Now we will address what parents need to know. If your child is being cyberbullied:

First, keep everything!

Your child needs to keep everything he receives or what is being posted online, no matter how much it hurts or embarrasses him. Place the harassment in a separate folder on the hard drive or CD, DVD, and so forth, and print a hard copy as well. You can also take a screen shot of anything sent to a smartphone or tablet and save it as a graphic file, as well as printing it. If you do not know how to do this, contact your cell phone provider or visit the smartphone manufacturer's website for instructions. If you need to take a screen shot on the computer, netbook, or laptop, the most common way is to go to the website page where the cyberbullying has been posted, then do the following for a PC:

Hit the PrtScrn or Print Screen key on the keyboard. Next, open Paint by going to the Start button, click on All Programs, then Accessories, then Paint. Once Paint opens, go to the Home tab in the Clipboard group, then select Paste. Save the file.

On a Mac or Apple computer:

Press the Command + Shift + 4 keys all at once, then move the crosshair pointer to where you want to start the screenshot. Drag to select the area you want to save, release your mouse or trackpad button, then look for the file (it will be .png) on your desktop and save it to the file you have created on your hard drive to save all the evidence.

Second, encourage your child to let you, a teacher, or another adult he trusts know about what is happening online. If he does, listen—he really wants you to try to understand. If you don't understand a social media site or app being used, ask him to show you or explain it. Again, listening is the big key here.

If you feel that he is not comfortable talking to you or another adult, let him know about Phoebe, the Cyber Crime Dog. She is a Siberian husky with blue eyes, the mascot of WHO@-KTD, and she can be contacted on the website at http://haltabusektd.org/phoebe/contact_phoebe.html. She also has her own Facebook profile at http://www.facebook.com/phoebe.crimedog, where they can become friends, or he can e-mail Phoebe at phoebe@halta-buse.org. He can read more about Phoebe at http://haltabusektd.org/phoebe/index.html and how she goes to schools to help teach students how to stay safer online.

If he still isn't comfortable, he can report cyberbullying (or bullying) anonymously at http://www.schooltipline.com. Find out if your child's school is listed on this site. If not, let the school principal, vice principal, counselor, or school resource officer know about it and encourage them to add the school to the site.

Third, make sure he contacts the person bothering him online *one* time via e-mail, post, or text with something as simple as "Please stop contacting me." Your child does not need to explain why, and reassure him that he is not being rude. CC (copy) the cyberbully's ISP (if you know it) and keep a copy of that e-mail, post, or text for your records.

Fourth, tell your child *not* to respond after that, but keep anything the cyberbully sends from that point forward.

Fifth, send complaints to the person's ISP with the full headers (if via e-mail). If you don't know how to do this, instructions are available at halta-busektd.org/help/headers/index.shtml.

Sixth, if someone has created a website, profile, or other account to harass your child, complain to the server where the site is hosted (WHO@-KTD can help).

Seventh, if the harassment/cyberbullying continues, go to WHO@-KTD for help at haltabusektd.org.

What If Your Child Is a Cyberbully?

- Know your school's policies about cyberbullying. Many are required by law to state its policies and procedures publicly. Some require students and parents to sign forms acknowledging awareness of the policies. Familiarize

Phoebe, the Cyber Crime Dog. Photo courtesy of Breathless Focus Photography.

yourself with the rules and discuss them with your children. If your child is accused of cyberbullying, make sure you understand your state's laws.

- Cooperate with school officials. Don't be quick to judge or shift blame for your child, the victim, or the school. Work with your school to understand what happened and your child's role. Cooperate to the extent you feel appropriate to resolve the issue to avoid the involvement of law enforcement.
- Be prepared: You may not get the full story. Your child and/or other children involved may give you a skewed version of what happened. School officials, anxious about potential litigation, may offer a different account of the incident, or be reluctant to become involved in an incident that may have occurred off campus, after school hours.
- Police may become involved, based on the severity of the incident and the number of students involved. You should cooperate fully with police and seek assistance of an attorney specializing in family law if your child is involved.
- The media may become involved. Local and national news media are reporting on bullying incidents as awareness and sensitivity to the problem grow. Victims' parents may grow impatient with their school and law enforcement and take their case to the media. Although many media have policies against naming minors in a story, the names of both cyberbullies and their victims have become public, then reported by the media, when other students reveal those names on social media, or when hacktivist groups do. Social media websites and search engines are being targeted through the legal system by parents of victims to reveal the names of cyberbullies who try to be anonymous.
- Find the source for your child's acting out. Is your child angry about a home situation such as a pending divorce or a parent who needs to work two or more jobs to make ends meet? Is he or she struggling with schoolwork? An underlying problem may call for counseling. Also, carefully examine your relationship with your child—are you modeling good interpersonal behaviors?
- Understand that you may need an attorney. Seek legal counsel immediately if the victim's parents announce their decision to file a lawsuit against the school and/or the alleged bully.

PARENTS NEED TO USE CYBER STREET SMARTS, TOO!

1. Learn to use the Internet better. Find out where your child goes online and go to those sites. If she has accounts on social media sites or apps, find

out which ones. Open an account yourself and ask to be a friend. Remind her that as long as she is under your roof, you want to make sure she is safe online. Promise that you will not snoop, or embarrass her if she friends you, and keep that promise.

2. Keep desktop or laptop computers in a central room in the house, such as the living room, family room, or kitchen, and make sure your child uses the computer there. Do not keep looking over her shoulder. She needs to be trusted to a certain extent and to know you won't be snooping on her.

3. As mentioned previously in this book, if your child has a laptop, tablet, or smartphone, set a cutoff time at night and you keep the device until morning. This will cut down on any drama that may be going on, and maybe she will get a good night's sleep!

4. Take advantage of "Smart Limits" or something similar that your cell phone provider may offer to give you more control over who contacts your child and who she can contact. Some cell phone providers also have controls to allow only a certain number of texts to be sent each month, block certain phone numbers, and more. Ask your cell phone provider what it offers.

5. Put filtering or monitoring software on any device your child uses. Until she leaves your house and is on her own, you have the right to keep track of what she is doing; if something happens, you can catch it before it grows out of proportion.

6. Check the history and cache on the computer she uses most often. If it's empty, then there is a problem. The most common way to check this is to open the Web browser, then hit the Ctrl + H keys at the same time. This brings up the history of the websites and pages your child has visited. You can then click on these to see what she was viewing. To check the cache in Microsoft Internet Explorer, go to the top right, click on Tools, then Internet Options, and a window will pop up. Go to Browsing History and click on Settings, then click on View Files. This should be filled with names of sites visited, any graphics, dates, and so on.

Parents also can use pledges—one showing what they will and will not do online regarding their kids, then one for their kids to sign pledging what they will and won't do online. Printable copies are available at http://halt abusektd.org/docs/safetypledgeP&G.pdf and http://haltabusektd.org/docs/ safetypledgeK&T.pdf; examples are noted below.

Finally, share this list of what is acceptable for your child (and you) to post online:

- Clean family photos
- Concerts, sporting events, or other entertainment you attend
- Party photos can be fun—be creative, not mean
- Vacations, trips to the beach or mountains, or just hanging out
- Interesting news links—about your favorite entertainer, movie, or music videos (keep it clean)
- It's okay to post that you're having a lousy day; just don't get too much into it. Everyone has a bad day or two!
- Family events such as the birth of a new baby, wedding, birthday, anniversary, or reunion
- Pics of your girlfriend or boyfriend (keep it clean)
- If you like to cook, post favorite recipes
- Your hobbies
- Video games you play and how you like or dislike them
- Positive things about your school (of course!)

Remember: Anytime anyone posts anything nasty on your wall, feed, blog, and so on, you have the right to remove the post and block the poster.

WHO@KTD

Working to Halt Online Abuse
Kids-Teen Division

Internet Safety Pledge for Kids and Teens

1. I will not give out any personal information such as my address, home/cell phone number, parents' work address/telephone number, or the name and location of my school without my parents' permission.

2. I will tell my parents right away if something or someone online makes me feel uncomfortable.

3. I will never agree to get together with someone I "met" online without first checking with my parents. If my parents agree to the meeting, I will be sure that it is in a public place and bring my mother or father or another trusted adult along.

4. I will never send a person my photo without first checking with my parents.

5. I will not respond to IMs, texts or emails that are mean or in any way make me feel uncomfortable. It is not my fault if I get a message like that. If I do I will tell my parents right away so that they can contact the Internet or cell service provider.

6. I will talk with my parents so that we can set up rules for going online. We will decide upon the time of day that I can be online, the length of time I can be online, and appropriate Web sites I can visit. I will not access unapproved Web sites without their permission.

7. I will not give out my Internet password to anyone (even my best friends) other than my parents.

8. I will check with my parents before downloading or installing software or doing anything that could possibly hurt our computer or jeopardize my family's privacy.

9. I will be a good netizen and will not do anything that hurts other people or is against the law.

10. I will help my parents understand how to have fun and learn things online and teach them things about the Internet, computers and other technology.

Signed

_____   _____
Kid/Teen   Parent/Guardian 1

_____
Parent/Guardian 2

For more information or help about cyberbulling, please contact WHOA KTD for help!

WHO@KTD

Working to Halt Online Abuse
Kids-Teen Division

haltabusektd.org

Kids' pledge.

WHO@KTD
Working to Halt Online Abuse
Kids-Teen Division

Internet Safety Pledge for Parents or Guardians

1. I will get to know what my child uses online (ie IM, chat, social networking, web chat, blogs, etc). If I don't know how to use them, I'll get my child to show me how.

2. I will set reasonable rules and guidelines for computer use by my children and will discuss these rules and post them near the computer as a reminder. I'll remember to monitor their compliance with these rules, especially when it comes to the amount of time they spend on the computer.

3. I will not overreact if my child tells me about a problem he or she is having on the Internet. Instead, we'll work together to try to solve the problem and prevent it from happening again.

4. I promise not to use the Internet as an electronic babysitter.

5. I will help make the Internet a family activity and ask my child to help plan family events using the Internet.

6. I will try to get to know my child's "online friends" just as I try get to know his or her other friends.

Signed

_____   _____
Parent/Guardian 1   Kid/Teen

_____
Parent/Guardian 2

For more information or help about cyberbulling, please contact WHOA KTD for help!

WHO@KTD
Working to Halt Online Abuse
Kids-Teen Division

haltabusektd.org

Parents' pledge.

CHAPTER THIRTEEN

Online Safety Tips, Resources, and Where to Go for Help

If your child is the victim of a cyberbully, here is a list of online safety tips to follow. A printable brochure in pdf format is available at WHO@-KTD with these tips:[1]

Use Cyber Street Smarts

- Don't trust everybody you meet online—even if they claim to be a "mutual friend."
- Only approve friends you really know—once they're approved, they can see *everything* you post online, including photos and videos.

KTDlarge.

- Be careful what you post online—it can and will be used against you. Employers and colleges/universities monitor social networking sites and do "Google" searches—you may lose a job or admission to the school of your dreams because of your online activity.
- Create a hard-to-guess password, such as m0n60o53 (mongoose), and *do not* share it with friends. You may be friends today but not tomorrow.
- Use a generic username/e-mail address. Never give your real name, age, address, workplace, or phone number online without permission from your parents/guardians.
- Use a free e-mail account such as Hotmail or Gmail for boards, blogs, chat rooms, social media, e-mails from strangers, and other online activities.
- Change your settings/preferences—the default usually allows everyone online and on that website to see everything you post; change it so that only your friends/buddies/followers can see what you do.
- Don't fill out surveys—they give other people more of your personal information.
- Don't take sexy photos of yourself to send to your boyfriend/girlfriend via cell phone or computer. They *will* land on the Internet for the world to see, and it's against the law.
- Lurk on groups, message boards, websites, blogs, and chat rooms before posting messages.
- When you do participate online, be careful—only type what you would say to someone's face.
- If you don't feel comfortable with someone who contacts you, do *not* respond. Block or ignore unwanted users. You're not being rude—your comfort level is more important than their feelings.
- Your first instinct may be to defend yourself if you are bothered online—don't. This is how most online harassment begins. And don't take revenge on someone online—it could land you in jail.

FILTERING AND MONITOR SOFTWARE FOR COMPUTERS AND SMARTPHONES

ComputerTime—http://www.softwaretime.com
Allows you to set limits on the amount of time and the time of day when children can use the computer.

Cyber Patrol—https://www.cyberpatrol.com
Allows you to manage computer use in your household.

Net Nanny—https://www.netnanny.com
    You can see and control access to websites and block sites you deem
    inappropriate.

PC Pandora—http://www.pcpandora.com
    Provides screenshots, keylogging, and more.

Norton Family Premier—http://us.norton.com/norton-family-premier
    Uses simple settings to make Web surfing safer, protects your child's infor-
    mation online, and protects multiple devices.

Phone Sheriff—http://www.phonesheriff.com
    Blocks phone numbers from calls and text messages, sets custom time
    restrictions and blocks apps you choose, monitors text messages, and gets
    custom activity alerts, real-time location tracking and lock commands;
    compatible with Android, iPhone, and iPad.

My Mobile Watchdog—https://www.mymobilewatchdog.com
    From the dashboard, access text messages, contacts, call logs; block apps
    and websites; locate your child; and much more.

My Social Sitter App—http://www.mysocialsitter.com
    My Social Sitter provides an instant filter before any social media message
    goes public.

AT&T SmartLimits—http://att.com/smartlimits
Verizon Parental Controls—http://www.internetsafetyproject.org/wiki/veri
    zon-parental-control-center
T-Mobile Content Lock—http://www.t-mobile.co.uk/help-and-advice/
    advice-for-parents/inappropriate-content
Sprint Parental Controls—http://support.sprint.com/support/service/cate
    gory/Parental_controls-Parental_controls
U.S. Cellular Family Protector—https://www.uscellular.com/uscellular/sup
    port/faq/faqD etails.jsp?topic = family-protector.html&parent = data
Ting Android Parental Controls—https://ting.com/blog/you-asked-android
    -parental-controls
iPhone Parental Controls—https://support.apple.com/en-us/HT201304
Virgin Mobile Parental Controls—http://parentalcontrols-on.org/Virgin
    -Mobile

The following organizations can help if your child is a victim of cyber–
bullying, sextortion, or other online issues:

WHO@-KTD (Kids/Teen Division)—www.haltabusektd.org
Established in September 2005 as an offshoot of WHO@, the KTD was designed to help kids and teens who are online victims of bullying, harassment, and stalking, in addition to educating them how to stay safer online. Parents, educators, and concerned adults will also find important information on the site, as well as the ability to get help for a kid or teen who is being bullied, harassed, or stalked online. Resources, research, and other helpful information is also available on the website.

Stand Up To Bullying logo.

Stand Up To Bullying—http://standuptobullying.net
This site provides some great resources, tips, and a chance to have a cyberbullying expert come to your school or event.

i-SAFE—www.isafe.org
The United States Congress designated i-SAFE America Inc., a nonprofit

isafe logo.

Internet safety foundation, to bring Internet safety education and awareness to the youth of this country. Founded in 1998, i-SAFE is a proactive
prevention-oriented Internet safety awareness program. It provides
Internet safety information and knowledge to students, parents, and
everyone in the community in a variety of ways.

The Institute for Responsible Online and Cell-Phone Communication—
http://www.iroc2.org
The Institute for Responsible Online and Cell-Phone Communication
(IROC2) is a 501(c)(3) nonprofit dedicated to constructing a global digital community free of negative and sometimes irreversible consequences
resulting from poor digital judgment. The Institute strives to achieve this
goal via its Course to Digital Consciousness by demonstrating that digital
activity—positive and negative—is public and permanent.

Cyberbullying Research Center—http://cyberbullying.org
The Cyberbullying Research Center is dedicated to providing up-to-date
information about the nature, extent, causes, and consequences of cyberbullying among adolescents. This website is a clearinghouse of information concerning the ways adolescents use and misuse technology. It is a
resource for parents, educators, law enforcement officers, counselors, and
others who work with youth. It includes facts, figures, and detailed stories
from those who have been impacted directly by online aggression. In addition, the site includes numerous resources to help prevent and respond to
cyberbullying incidents.

School Tipline—http://www.schooltipline.com
SchoolTipline Inc., the leader in school incident reporting and emergency alerts, delivers solutions that open communication and reduce vio-
lence and other destructive behavior at school that may adversely affect a
culture of learning and safety. SchoolTipline enables school administrators to use students as their eyes and ears to detect, identify, and report
incidents in their earliest stages.

IROC2.

Interpol—http://www.interpol.int/Member-countries/World

INTERPOL has a global membership of 190 countries. Each country maintains a National Central Bureau (NCB) staffed by national law enforcement officers. It forms the link with INTERPOL's global network, enabling member countries to work together on cross-border investigations. NCBs are increasingly involved in shaping the organization's direction. Their role is to enable police around the world to work together to make the world a safer place. Interpol's high-tech infrastructure of technical and operational support helps meet the growing challenges of fighting crime in the twenty-first century.

Cyberbullying Research Center logo.

ThinkUKnow—https://www.thinkuknow.co.uk, http://www.thinkuknow.org.au
  ThinkUKnow is a free, evidence-based program that provides accessible cyber safety education to parents, guardians, and teachers through schools and organizations across Australia and the United Kingdom. ThinkUKnow uses a network of trained law enforcement members and accredited volunteers from its program partner organizations to deliver cyber safety education presentations nationwide.

NetSmartz—http://www.netsmartz.org
  NetSmartz Workshop is an interactive, educational program of the National Center for Missing & Exploited Children® (NCMEC) that provides age-appropriate resources to help teach children how to be safer on- and offline. The program is designed for children ages five to seventeen, parents and guardians, educators, and law enforcement. With resources such as videos, games, activity cards, and presentations, NetSmartz entertains while it educates.

Stopbullying.gov—http://www. stopbullying.gov
  StopBullying.gov provides information from various government agencies on what bullying is, what cyberbullying is, who is at risk, and how to prevent and respond to bullying.

CyberBullyHelp—http://cyberbullyhelp.com
  Provides information about cyberbullying, offers help and resources, as well as information about training and presentations.

stopbullying.gov

Stopbullying.

Delete Cyberbullying—http://www.deletecyberbullying.org
This site aims to educate parents and teens about the dangers of living in a connected world. Explore the site and join in the fight to stop online harassment.

Social Media Sites/Apps Offering Safety Information for Users

This is just a short list. To find more, search online for the website or app with "safety" after it, such as "Facebook Safety."

Ask.fm—http://safety.ask.fm
ASK.fm's Safety Center is full of information to help get the most out of its service in a safer, more positive way.

Twitter Safety & Security for Kids and Teens—https://about.twitter.com/safety/teens
Privacy and security are important topics, especially because by default, *anyone* can see your tweets. It breaks down privacy and security settings so you can take control of your experience.

Facebook Family Safety Center—https://www.facebook.com/safety
It views safety as a conversation and a shared responsibility among all of us. You will find information, tools, and resources there.

Snapchat Safety Center—https://www.snapchat.com/safety
Together with its safety advisory board, some of the world's leading safety advocates, it has developed guides for staying safe while using Snapchat. Within its safety center parents, teachers, and Snapchatters can find safety tips, research, and resources.

ask.fm logo.

Twitter logo.

facebook logo.

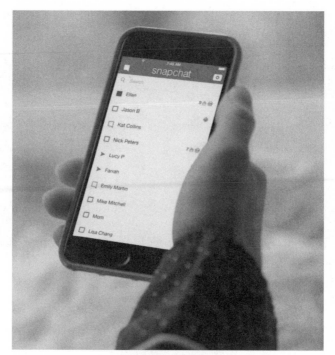

Snapchatpressphoto.

Instagram Tips for Parents—https://help.instagram.com/154475974694511
 How Instagram works, and tips and advice.

Skype Safety & Security—http://www.skype.com/en/security
 Protecting your online safety, security, and privacy.

Kik's Safety Guide for Parents—http://blog.kik.com/2016/02/04/kiks-safety
-guide-for-paents
 Tips from the guide to make sure parents and teens have the best possible
 experience on Kik.

Periscope Help Center—https://help.periscope.tv/
 Covers inappropriate content, harassing or abuse behavior, and who to
 contact for help (type "safety" in the search box for proper results).

Skype logo.

Kik logo.

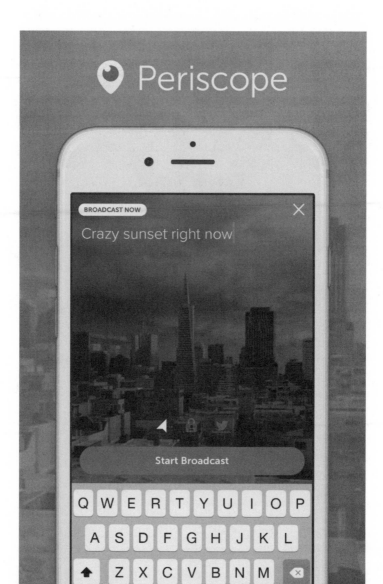

Periscope logo.

Glossary

Acceptable Usage Policy. Also known as an AUP or terms of service used by ISPs, social networking sites, and the like. When you open an account, you need to accept this before your account can be created. It outlines the conditions of your use of that site/application.

Apps. Applications for use on smartphones and tablets, these small, specialized programs make it easier to access their content.

Blog. Web log or online journal/diary, usually located on a website (such as blogger.com or livejournal.com) or on a personal website.

Bookmark. Marking and saving a favorite website URL; it makes it possible to return to that site without doing a search for it.

Bounce. When an e-mail message is returned to you as being undeliverable or another error, indicating a problem with the recipient's account.

Broadband. A wide band of frequency used for telecommunications; used when describing either DSL or a cable connection to the Internet.

Browser. A program used to view sites/pages on the World Wide Web. Popular browsers are Firefox, Google Chrome, Opera, and Microsoft Internet Explorer.

Cable. High-speed Internet access through a cable service provider.

Cache. A folder/area on a hard drive where frequently accessed data is stored, such as the website URLs and pages you've visited plus the cookies and graphics associated with them. The information in your cache allows your Web browser to access a website faster if you have visited it in the past, unless you have deleted the cache.

Chat. Real-time or live conversation online. This happens in a virtual room with a few, one hundred, or even more online users. Or it can happen one-on-one in a private room.

Cookies. Information files stored on the hard drive by your Web browser when you visit certain websites. This information is used to keep track of, for example, the last time you visited that website, what you ordered, or where it was mailed. Each cookie is different. Some may have basic information, such as your last visit; others may have a lot more information, including what kind of computer you use, the name of your ISP, and your full name, address, and telephone number. Not all websites "set" cookies (save them to your hard drive). Most firewall/security programs allow you to delete these cookies if you wish. Cookies are used to store your logged-in sessions. These store your username and a special encoded key for the session, such as when you check the "Keep me logged in" box on a website.

Cyberbully/cyberbullying. When offline bullying goes to the Internet, mainly via instant messaging (IM) and cell phone text messaging, primarily targeted at school-age children, literally giving them nowhere to hide from their bullies.

Cyberspace. Coined by author William Gibson in his novel *Neuromancer*, this refers to the Internet or World Wide Web and the culture it spawned.

Cyberstalking. When one form of online harassment leads to other forms, then to an obsession with the victim, sometimes culminating in real-life stalking and harassment.

DNS (Domain Name System). A database system that translates a domain name into an IP address. For example, a domain name such as www.comset.net converts to the numeric address 213.172. 9.119.

Domain. The Internet is divided into smaller sets known as domains, including .com (business), .gov (government), .edu (educational), .mil (military), .org (nonprofit organizations), .net (miscellaneous organizations), and more.

Domain Name. This identifies the website and consists of two parts: the first is the registered name of the site, the second is the sub-domain or category. Take, for example, the website address usmc.mil. The "usmc" is the United States Marine Corps website and ".mil" is the military category. Put together, they form the domain name.

DSL (Digital Subscriber Line). Available through the telephone company, it allows high-speed access to the Internet through your telephone landline.

Ego Surf. To search online for yourself as a safety precaution to make sure more information isn't out there than you want. Here's the best way to ego-surf: put your name in quotes in a search engine, such as "jayne hitchcock," then check the results to see on which sites/pages you may be listed. This gives you a refined list of results, rather than getting too many.

E-Mail. An e-mail address consists of the username, then the "@" (called an "at" sign), the name of the Internet service provider (ISP), and the domain, or the designation the ISP has been assigned. In the e-mail address "Janice@hotmail.com," the breakdown is: "Janice" is the username, "hotmail" is the ISP, and ".com" is the domain category.

Emoji. Graphics that depict different facial expressions, sentiments, or ideas. Usually added to comments or posts on social media or via smartphone texts.

Emoticon. A combination of characters that form a facial expression, of sorts, when looked at sideways. For example, the characters :) make a smile or, in Net terms, a smiley. Often used in e-mail and newsgroup messages, as well as chat rooms.

FAQ (Frequently Asked Questions). A collection of the most frequently asked questions and answers on a particular subject or about a website, TV show, product, and so forth.

Feedback. Found mostly in online auctions, the seller and winning bidder can leave feedback or comments for each other when an auction sale is completed. Feedback results can be viewed by anyone prior to making a bid to check whether the seller or bidder has had a positive, neutral, or negative experience.

Firewall. Protection for computer systems, tablets, smartphones, networks, and so on from attacks by hackers, viruses, Trojans, and more, in either hardware or software form.

Full Headers. Additional information found in e-mail and messages that denotes where a message originates, even if someone forges the return e-mail address or uses a free e-mail account such as Hotmail.

GIF (Graphic Information Format). A common format used for photos or graphics.

Harassment. Badgering, annoying, worrying, or tormenting another person, often through repeated unwelcome contact. Online harassment typically occurs when someone begins sending nasty messages via e-mail, chat, social media, or message boards. If not stopped at this stage, it could lead to cyberstalking.

Header. What you usually see in an e-mail message or Usenet post: the TO:, FROM:, DATE:, and SUBJECT: lines. See Full Headers.

History: Text file that lists all the websites you visited with your Web browser. Usually it can be accessed while using the browser and hitting the Ctrl + H keys.

Home Page. The first page of a website (also known as index.html). Or, the website/page that automatically loads each time you launch your browser.

HTML (HyperText Markup Language). Web pages are made of it. Tags that make what you see look "pretty." Example: I am here would make those words show up in bold type: I am here. If you're not familiar with HTML, go to a website/page, right-click your mouse, click on "View Source," and you'll see what looks like a different language. Anything in "arrows" is the HTML code.

HTTP (HyperText Transfer Protocol). Seen at the beginning of a URL, this is a set of instructions for communication between a server and a site.

HTTPS. This means you've gone to a website that is secure, allowing for safe online transactions, whether it's shopping, banking, or a protected site that only certain people can access.

Identity Theft. When someone steals your identity online, impersonates you, and wreaks havoc in your name—many times charging money to credit cards you never received, taking out loans, and ordering items, or worse.

Internet. A worldwide set of computers using TCP/IP; the World Wide Web is a subset of these computers.

Intranet. Similar to a local area network (LAN). An internal Internet available only to those within that company or building.

IP (Internet Protocol). How data is sent from one computer (aka a "host") to another on the Internet. This is the most popular of protocols on which the Internet is based. Each host has at least one IP address that uniquely identifies it from all other hosts on the Internet. See IP Address.

IP Address (Internet Protocol Address). A set of four numbers with three numerals in each set that identify where you are located. Every computer/server has a unique number, so if you use a dial-up ISP, you may have a different IP address each time you dial in to the Internet, as ISPs run more than one server to accommodate their customers. The larger the ISP, the more servers, thus more IP addresses. So one day you may log in to an IP address of 204.52.190.0, the next day you might log in to an IP address of 204.52.191.2. If you have cable Internet, you are assigned one IP address, which can be traced back to you (or the account holder).

ISP (Internet Service Provider). Also called an IAP (Internet Access Provider), a company that provides access to the Internet.

IT. Information Technology.

JPEG (Joint Photographic Experts Group) or JPG. Most commonly used format for graphics and photos. Opens in just about any graphics program.

Login. When you sign into your account, profile, or other online persona.

Lurker. Someone who is present in an online forum but doesn't chat or post, just reads the conversation going on around him. This is called "lurking."

Meme (Internet). This is a video, graphic, post, or other online material that goes viral. Sometimes people will change the message so many versions will be online. One example is planking—a person has a photo taken of him lying down horizontally in a public place or unusual place.

Netiquette. To be polite online.

Netizens. Common nickname for online users.

Newbie. Someone new to the Internet.

Network. A system of connected computers exchanging information with each other.

Online. When you connect to your ISP or Wi-Fi, you are online. Anything you do related to this is considered being online, whether it's sending e-mail, surfing websites, chatting, or reading message boards.

Password. Used to protect your accounts. It is extremely important to make sure your password is a combination of letters and numbers (also symbols, if possible), so that it is hard for someone to guess and gain access to your account. Passwords should be changed regularly for safety purposes.

PDF (Portable Document Format). A file in .pdf format is commonly opened in Adobe Acrobat. Used for fillable forms, brochures, handouts, and so forth.

Post. To send a message online in social media, on a message board, or other online forum. You use links or click on graphical buttons that read something like "Post a new message/subject" or "Reply to this topic/subject." Each forum has a different way to post.

Preference Settings (Options). Where you can select the options you want in your browser, e-mail, newsreader, and IM programs.

Profile. All about you, depending on how much information you input. Popular with social media websites and apps. Remember, the less information you provide, the less likely you'll become an online victim. Don't give away too much.

Screen Name. See Username.

Scroll. When on a website, to scroll, place your mouse cursor on the bar on the far right or bottom of the screen and move the bar down or up to go to a different part of a Web page; the page up/page down or a scroll button on a mouse can be used to do this as well.

Search Engine. A tool for searching for information on the Internet by topic. Popular search engines include Yahoo!, Google, and Bing. Type in your search query using one or more words.

Server. A computer connected to the Internet that stores and/or provides information, such as Web pages, e-mail messages, and posts.

Sexting. Send seminude, nude, or provocative photos via smartphone, cell phone, tablet, computer, or other electronic device to another person.

Site. A single page or collection of related Web pages at one domain.

Smiley. See Emoticons.

Snail Mail. The U.S. Postal Service delivers this to your house six days a week.

Social Networking. Websites or smartphone apps where people can connect and post comments, photos, or videos. Common ones are Facebook, Twitter, Snapchat, and Instagram.

Spam. Unsolicited electronic junk mail, advertisements, or offers, usually unwanted by the receiver.

Spyware. An independent, executable program on a computer, usually put there without the computer user's knowledge.

Surf. Common term for going from site to site or page to page on the Web.

Swatting. When the loser of an online video game or someone getting revenge calls in a false 911 call to the victim's location to see how large the law enforcement response is.

Techie. Someone who is a computer and/or Internet expert.

Texting. Also known as Text Messaging, mostly associated with cell or smartphones. Texts are sent from your cell phone or smartphone to another person's phone.

TOS (Terms of Service). The rules and regulations an ISP, website host, or forum implements; its users must abide by the rules or risk being kicked off or denied access to the service.

Trash. Usually a function in e-mail programs that allows the user to delete unwanted e-mail, thus putting it in the trash; usually the trash empties when the user exits or ends use of the e-mail program.

UCE (Unsolicited Commercial E-mail). More commonly known as electronic junk mail or spam.

URL (Uniform Resource Locator). A Web address or location. For example, www.ja hitchcock.com would be the URL for my personal website.

Username (also user ID or screen name). What you select or are given to use as your ID online. Example: anotherwriter@hotmail.com—"anotherwriter" is my username/user ID for my Hotmail account. It's always good to select a gender-neutral username.

Virus. A program that infects your computer. Can range from being only a nuisance and cause "snow" to fall on your screen or "dancing animals" to appear, to being a serious threat that damages your files and hard drive. Some viruses have been known to completely wipe a hard drive clean. The most famous virus was Melissa, which appeared on computers worldwide in 1999.

Webcam. A camera attached to your computer used to transmit images over the Internet to others who have a Webcam, in Webcam chat rooms, Skype, ooVoo, and so forth.

Web Host. A site that allows users to join/subscribe and receive a host of services, such as personal Web page space, e-mail accounts, chat, message boards, and more, usually for free. Web hosts are available to people who already have online access through an ISP.

WWW. World Wide Web, or simply, the Web.

Notes

Foreword

1. 11 Facts about Cyberbullying, *DoSomething.org*.
2. Cyberbullying Statistics 2014, *NoBullying.com*, December 22, 2015.
3. Rep. Katherine Clark, "Sexism in Cyberspace," *The Hill*, March 10, 2015.
4. Hayley Tsukayama, "Online Abuse Is a Real Problem. This Congresswoman Wants the FBI To Treat It Like One," *Washington Post*, June 7, 2015.
5. Callum Borchers and Jack Newsham, "In a First, Healey Files Criminal Cyber-Harassment Charges," *Boston Globe*, July 17, 2015.

Chapter 1

1. Amanda Todd, "My Story: Struggling, Bullying, Suicide, Self Harm," October 11, 2012, https://www.youtube.com/watch?v=ej7afkypUsc.
2. "Man Charged in Netherlands in Amanda Todd Suicide Case," *BBC News*, April 18, 2014, http://www.bbc.com/news/world-europe-27076991.
3. Working to Halt Online Abuse—Kids/Teen Division, http://www.haltabusektd.org.
4. Cox Communications Teen Online & Wireless Safety Survey: Cyberbullying, Sexting, and Parental Controls in Partnership with the National Center for Missing & Exploited Children® (NCMEC) and John Walsh, May 2009, http://www.cox.com/wcm/en/aboutus/datasheet/takecharge/2009-teen-survey.pdf?campcode=takecharge-research-link_2009-teen-survey_0511.
5. Janice D'Arcy. "Sioux City Journal Editorial Shines a Light on Bullying Same Weekend 'Bully' Comes Out." *Washington Post*, April 23, 2012, https://www.washingtonpost.com/blogs/on-parenting/post/sioux-city-journal-editorial-shines-a-light-on-bullying-same-weekend-bully-comes-out/2012/04/23/gIQAmr0FcT_blog.html. Retrieved March 21, 2016.

6. "Kenneth Weishuhn, Gay Iowa Teen, Commits Suicide after Allegedly Receiving Death Threats." *Huffington Post*, April 17, 2012, http://www.huffingtonpost.com/2012/04/17/kenneth-weishuhn-gay-iow a-teen-suicide_n_1431442.html. Retrieved March 21, 2016.

7. "Iowa Mom Blames Gay Teen Son's Suicide on Bullying." *Fox News*, April 18, 2012, http://www.foxnews.com/us/2012/04/18/iowa-mom-blames-gay-teen-son-suicide -on-bullying.html. Retrieved March 21, 2016.

8. Nobody Knows Me (MDNA Tour Interlude/Backdrop, 2012), Madonna, https://vimeo.com/45542445. Retrieved March 21, 2016.

9. Facebook profile of Kenneth Weishuhn Jr., https://www.facebook.com/Kenneth Weishuhn97.

10. Remember Kenneth James Weishuhn Jr., https://www.facebook.com/groups/359685704081860.

11. Cyberbullying Facts and Statistics That You Need to Know, Florence, Ing, June 6, 2014, https://blog.udemy.com/cyberbullying-facts.

12. "What is Cyberbullying?" Nobullying.com, December 22, 2015, http://nobullying .com/what-is-cyberbullying.

13. "What is a Burner Phone?," February 19, 2015, https://www.puretalkusa.com/blog/what-is-a-burner-phone. Retrieved February 4, 2016.

14. U.S. Court of Appeals, United States of America, *Plaintiff-Appellee, v. Melvin Skinner*, Defendant-Appellant, August 12, 2012, http://www.ca6.uscourts.gov/opinions .pdf/12a0262p-06.pdf.

15. Teens and Cyberbullying, National Crime Prevention Council (NCPC), February 28, 2007, http://www.ncpc.org/resources/files/pdf/bullying/Teens%20and%20Cyberbully ing%20Research%20Study.pdf.

16. The Institute for Responsible Online and Cell Phone Communication (IROC2), www.iroc2.org.

Chapter 2

1. "Mom Loses Daughter over 'Sexting,' Demands Accountability," WLWT5 TV, October 12, 2009, http://www.wlwt.com/Mom-Loses-Daughter-Over-Sexting-Demands -Accountability/26949706. Retrieved December 12, 2015.

2. "Mom Loses Daughter Over 'Sexting,' Demands Accountability."

3. Civil complaint and jury demand. Filed December 2, 2009, http://www.wired.com/images_blogs/threatlevel/2009/12/logan-sexting-suit.pdf.

4. "Family of Jessica Logan, Who Hanged Herself after Nude-Picture Sexting Led to Bullying, Awarded $154,000 in Settlement," *New York Daily News*, October 12, 2009, http://www.nydailynews.com/news/national/teen-bullying-victim-family-settlement-art icle-1.1178783. Retrieved October 14, 2015.

5. The Impact of House Bill 116 on Your School District, Ohio School Plan, http://www.ohioschoolplan.org/03-13-12.html.

6. "What is Cyberbullying?," Stopbullying.gov, http://www.stopbullying.gov/cyber bullying/what-is-it.

7. Summary of our Cyberbullying Research (2004–2015), Cyberbullying.org, http://cyberbullying.org/summary-of-our-cyberbullying-research.

8. Shared Stories of Cyberbullying, Cyberbullying Research Center, http://cyber bullying.org/stories.

Chapter 3

1. "Mother of 17-year-old Rehtaeh Parsons Who Killed Herself over Cyber Bullying Pens Heart-wrenching Message to the Teen Who Sent Naked Pictures of Her Daughter to Friends," Dailymail.co.uk, January 18, 2015, http://www.dailymail.co.uk/news/article-2916543/Mother-17-year-old-Rehtaeh-Parsons-killed-cyber-bullying-pens-heart-wrenching-message-boy-sent-naked-pictures-daughter-friends.html#ixzz3x9Gkv2yt. Retrieved August 21, 2015.

2. "The Man Who Texted a Photo of Himself Having Sex with a Girl While She Vomited Isn't Getting Any Jail Time," Vice.com, January 18, 2015, http://www.vice.com/read/no-jail-time-for-man-who-texted-photo-of-himself-penetrating-rehtaeh-parsons-while-she-vomited-273. Retrieved August 21, 2015.

3. "The Man Who Texted a Photo of Himself Having Sex with a Girl While She Vomited Isn't Getting Any Jail Time."

4. "Nova Scotia Cyberbullying Law Inspired by Rehtaeh Parsons Case Struck Down," *Huffington Post Canada*, December 11, 2015, http://www.huffingtonpost.ca/2015/12/11/rehtaeh-parsons-law-struc k-down_n_8785226.html. Retrieved August 21, 2015.

5. Joseph Yeager, Parents Guide to Social Media Facebook Group, https://www.face book.com/ParentsGuidetoSocialMedia.

6. Case JE-49, Court of Appeals Georgia, October 10, 2014, https://efast.gaappeals.us/download?filingId=02f15598-53cc-4eb2-8707-3ad3c3c90676.

7. http://cyberbullying.us/state-cyberbullying-laws-a-brief-review-of-state-cyberbul lying-laws-and-policies; S. Hinduja and J. Patchin. *State Cyberbullying Laws: A Brief Review of State Cyberbullying Laws and Policies*. Cyberbullying Research Center, 2015. Retrieved August 25, 2015, from http://cyberbullying.org/Bullying-and-Cyberbullying-Laws.pdf.

8. Working to Halt Online Abuse, Cyberstalking Laws, http://www.haltabuse.org/resources/laws.

9. "Cyberstalking: A New Challenge for Law Enforcement and Industry: A Report from the Attorney General to the Vice President." Washington, DC: U.S. Department of Justice, 1999. NCJ 179575.

10. Quote from an e-mail interview with the author.

Chapter 4

1. Asperger's Syndrome by the Autism Society, http://www.autism-society.org/what-is/aspergers-syndrome.

2. Personal interview by the author.

3. https://www.bitstrips.com.

4. http://www.elsforautismcanada.com/stories.html, Ernie Els for Autism website.

5. Personal interview by the author.

6. "'Heil Hitler' Photo Lands Greely Girls in Hot Water," *Portland Press Herald*, February 6, 2013, http://www.pressherald.com/2013/02/06/photo-lands-greely-girls-in-hot-water_2013-02-07. Retrieved September 3, 2015.

7. "Can Twitter Help Rape Victims Find Justice?," July 23, 2012, http://www.slate.com/blogs/xx_factor/2012/07/23/savannah_dietrich_outs_her_rapists_on_twitter_and_facebook.html. Retrieved September 14, 2016.

8. Monteagle Elementary School Bullying/Harassment/Intimidation Policy, August 4, 2012, http://www.monteagleelementary.org/?PageName = LatestNews&Section = Spotlight&ItemID = 22010&ISrc = School&Itype = Spotlight&SchoolID = .

9. http://net-force.net.

10. "What's the School's Role in This?," Stopcyberbullying.org, http://www.stopcyberbullying.org/prevention/schools_role.html.

Chapter 5

1. https://ask.fm.

2. "Confessions of a Cyberbully," Netdoctor.co.uk, February 18, 2014, http://www.netdoctor.co.uk/parenting/teenager/a9270/confessions-of-a-cyberbully. Retrieved October 13, 2015.

3. "Hanna Smith Suicide Fuels Calls for Action on Ask.fm Cyberbullying," *CNN*, August 9, 2013, http://www.cnn.com/2013/08/07/world/europe/uk-social-media-bullying. Retrieved October 13, 2015.

4. "Confessions of a Cyberbully."

5. "Is My Child a Cyberbully?," PureSight Online Child Safety, http://puresight.com/Cyberbullying/is-my-child-a-victim.html.

6. "Mother Has No Regrets over Exposing Her Daughter as a Cyber Bully," January 14, 2014, http://metro.co.uk/2014/01/14/mother-has-no-regrets-over-exposing-daughter-as-cyber-bully-4262655/#ixzz43Z3aqakp. Retrieved March 19, 2016.

7. "My Child Is a Cyberbully, What Do I Do?," http://www.webroot.com/us/en/home/resources/tips/cyberbullying-online-predators/safety-my-child-is-a-cyberbully-what-do-i-do.

8. Internet Filter Software Reviews, 2016 Best, http://internet-filter-review.toptenreviews.com.

9. http://www.netsmartz.org/parents.

10. http://www.thinkuknow.org.au.

11. http://www.meganmeierfoundation.org.

12. "The Suicide of Phoebe Prince," January 30, 2016, https://en.wikipedia.org/wiki/Suicide_of_Phoebe_Prince. Retrieved March 21, 2016.

13. "Tyler's Story," nd, http://www.tylerclementi.org/tylers-story.

Chapter 6

1. Personal interview with the author.

2. Personal interview with the author.

3. http://www.haltabusektd.org.

4. Personal interview with the author.

5. A popular anonymous "ask me anything" site at the time.

6. A microblogging platform and website.

7. Emotional, sensitive, shy, introverted, or angst-ridden, Wikipedia, https://en.wikipedia.org/wiki/Emo, March 6, 2016. Retrieved March 21, 2016.

8. Personal interview with the author.

9. http://www.bulliedtosilence.com.

10. http://theveayotwins.com.

11. https://youtu.be/2psotWErj_Y.

Chapter 7

1. Name was changed for anonymity.

2. Name was changed for anonymity.

3. How To Send DMCA Notifications, http://www.seologic.com/faq/dmca-notifications.

4. Name was changed for anonymity.

5. http://www.kik.com.

6. Sextortion: Questions & Answers, September 16, 2015, http://www.interpol.int/content/download/24615/340944/version/14/file/2015.09.16%20-%20E%20-%20Sextortion%20Q%20and%20A.pdf. Retrieved November 9, 2015.

7. http://www.skype.com/en.

8. "Bid to Extradite Man over Daniel Perry 'Sextortion' Death," BBC News, February 18, 2016, http://www.bbc.com/news/uk-scotland-edinburgh-east-fife-35603933. Retrieved March 21, 2016.

9. "Coordinated Operation Strikes Back at 'Sextortion' Networks," May 2, 2014, http://www.interpol.int/News-and-media/News/2014/N2014-075. Retrieved August 31, 2015.

10. "Philippines Link to Blackmail Death of Scots Teenager," The Herald, May 2, 2014, http://www.heraldscotland.com/news/13158511.Philippines_link_to_blackmail_death_of_Scots_teenager. Retrieved March 21, 2016.

11. Sextortion, July 7, 2015, https://www.fbi.gov/news/stories/2015/july/sextortion. Retrieved August 31, 2015.

12. Sextortion: Questions & Answers.

Chapter 8

1. www.myspace.com.

2. https://itunes.apple.com/us/genre/ios-social-networking/id6005?mt = 8.

3. Name changed for anonymity.

4. Name changed for anonymity.

5. Name changed for anonymity.

6. Personal interview with the author.

7. "Now We've Seen Secret's Ugly Soul, Will Investors Act?," Pando.com, August 3, 2014, https://pando.com/2014/08/03/now-weve-seen-secrets-ugly-soul-will-investors-act. Retrieved August 31, 2015.

8. http://www.your-voice.org, sponsored by Whisper.

9. "Ralston Superintendent Shares Message of Hope after Son's Suicide," KETV 7 Philadelphia, January 31, 2016, http://www.ketv.com/news/ralston-superintendent-shares -message-of-hope-after-sons-suicide/37742958. Retrieved March 1, 2016.

10. Personal interview with the author.

11. "Facebook's Suicide Prevention Tool Launches in the UK: Alert System Offers Advice and Support to Concerned Users, February 19, 2016," http://www.dailymail.co.uk/ sciencetech/article-3454277/Facebook-s-Suicide-Prevention-tool-launches-UK-Alert -offers-advice-support-concerned-users.html. Facebook's Suicide Prevention tool launches in the UK: Alert system offers advice and support to concerned users, Post February 19, 2016, Retrieved February 23, 2016.

12. https://support.twitter.com/articles/15794#.

13. Institute for Responsible Online and Cell-Phone Communication, www.iroc2.org.

14. Personal interview with the author.

15. "The Acronyms Teens Really Use On Social Media," CNN, October 6, 2015, http:// www.cnn.com/2015/10/02/health/acronyms-teens-social-media-being13/index.html. Re-trieved November 9, 2015.

Chapter 9

1. Name change for anonymity.

2. Name change for anonymity.

3. Commonwealth of Massachusetts Office of the District Attorney, Common-wealth's Response to Defendant's Motion to Dismiss, Indictment No. 15YO0001NE, August 21, 2015 (publicly available document).

4. "Court Rules Massachusetts Teen Michelle Carter Must Stand Trial for Encouraging Boyfriend's Suicide," nydailynews.com, July 1, 2016, http://www.nydailynews.com/news/

crime/michelle-carter-ordered-stand-trial-boyfriend-suicide-article-1.2696249. Retrieved July 27, 2016.

5. *Sherman v. McDonald's*, Matthews Management Company and Aaron Brummley, *On Point News*, Case No. CV-2008-4379-4, civil suit, November 21, 2008, http://www.on pointnews.com/docs/nudephotos.pdf.

6. Smartphone Security, https://usa.kaspersky.com/internet-security-center/internet -safety/smartphones#.VtchxUBykms.

7. "Do You Need Help with an Identity Theft Problem?," http://www.idtheftcenter.org/ Fact-Sheets/fs-144.html.

Chapter 10

1. Gamergate Controversy, Wikipedia, March 21, 2016, https://en.wikipedia.org/ wiki/Gamergate_controversy. Retrieved March 21, 2016.

2. Swatting, Wikipedia, March 20, 2016, https://en.wikipedia.org/wiki/Swatting. Retrieved March 20, 2016.

3. "Teen Who Posted Viral 'Damn Daniel' Video Victim of Swatting," *Eyewitness News ABC 7*, New York, February 23, 2016, http://abc7ny.com/news/teen-who-posted -viral-damn-daniel-video-victim-of-swatting/1214672. Retrieved March 1, 2016.

4. Don't Make the Call: The New Phenomenon of Swatting, FBI website, February 2, 2008, https://www.fbi.gov/news/stories/2008/february/swatting020408. Retrieved January 4, 2016.

5. Last Defendant Sentenced in Swatting Controversy, FBI website, November 16, 2009, https://www.fbi.gov/dallas/press-releases/2009/dl111609.htm. Retrieved January 4, 2016.

6. Battlefield 4 description, Wikipedia, November 4, 2015, https://en.wikipedia.org/ wiki/Battlefield_4. Retrieved November 9, 2015.

7. "15 Year Old Who 'SWATTED' Gamer Convicted of Domestic Terrorism; 25 Years to Life in Federal Prison," *National Report*, March 20, 2015, http://national report.net/15-year-old-swatted-domestic-terrorism. Retrieved January 15, 2016.

8. Don't Make the Call: The New Phenomenon of Swatting, February 2, 2008, FBI .gov, https://archives.fbi.gov/archives/news/stories/2008/february/swatting020408. Re- trieved January 4, 2016.

9. "Teen Who 'Swatted' Disneyland Had Too Much Time on Hands," *CBC Canada*, June 30, 2015, http://www.cbc.ca/news/canada/british-columbia/teen-who-swatted-dis neyland-had-too-much-time-on-hands-1.3132444. Retrieved November 7, 2015.

10. "Australia's First Public Swatting Victim a Nice Bloke," *The Register*, June 5, 2014, http://www.theregister.co.uk/2014/06/05/australias_first_public_swat_victim_a_nice_ bloke. Retrieved November 9, 2015.

11. http://hackforums.net.

12. Rep. Clark's Interstate Swatting Bill, September 25, 2015, https://drive.goo gle.com/file/d/0B-QkCUPMetwXemFNYlZvOW4zaVk/view. Retrieved January 4, 2016.

13. "Police Swarm Katherine Clark's Home after Apparent Hoax," *Boston Globe*, February 1, 2016, https://www.bostonglobe.com/metro/2016/02/01/cops-swarm-rep-kathe
rine-clark-melrose-home-after-apparent-hoax/yqEpcpWmKtN6bOOAj8FZXJ/story.html.
Retrieved March 1, 2016.

Chapter 11

1. Personal interview conducted by the author.
2. Name changed for anonymity.

Chapter 12

1. Cyberbullying Scenarios, http://cyberbullying.org/cyberbullying-scenarios.
2. S. Hinduja and J. W. Patchin. *Bullying Beyond the Schoolyard: Preventing and Responding to Cyberbullying*, 2nd ed. (Thousand Oaks, CA: Sage Publications, 2015).
3. Resources for Educators, http://cyberbullying.org/resources/educators.
4. S. Hinduja and J. W. Patchin Cyberbullying Fact Sheet: Identification, Prevention, and Response, 2014. Cyberbullying Research Center. Retrieved 2016 from http://cyber
bullying.org/Cyberbullying_Identification_Prevention_Response.pdf.
5. S. Hinduja and J. Patchin. Preventing Cyberbullying: Top Ten Tips for Educators. Cyberbullying Research Center, 2014. Retrieved 2016 from http://cyberbullying.org/Top
-Ten-Tips-Educators-Cyberbullying-Prevention.pdf.

Chapter 13

1. http://haltabusektd.org/docs/ktddangers.pdf, online safety printable handout.

Index

About the Author

J. A. Hitchcock is a nationally recognized cybercrime and cyberbullying expert who has helped pass laws related to online harassment in many states, including Maryland, Minnesota, Michigan, Maine, Rhode Island, and New Hampshire. As president of Working to Halt Online Abuse (WHO@, at www. haltabuse.org), J. A. helps victims of cyberstalking crimes fight back. She volunteers as a consultant on Internet crime cases for police departments worldwide, the U.S. Department of Justice Victims of Crime, and the National Center for Victims of Crime.

Hitchcock also gives presentations to educators, librarians, corporations, and the public about staying safer online, as well as to students from the fourth grade through the college and university level. Her expertise has been used in media coverage of cyberstalking and related topics in *Time*, the *Los Angeles Times*, *Boston Globe*, *Ladies Home Journal*, *Glamour*, *Cosmopolitan*, and the Associated Press newswire. She has appeared on television on many news and related shows including *Primetime Thursday*, *48 Hours*, *A&E Investigative Reports*, *Inside Edition*, *Good Morning America*, and *Unsolved Mysteries*.

Hitchcock received the 2015 Mary Litynski Award from Messaging, Malware and Mobile Anti-Abuse Working Group (M³AAWG) for her work in online abuse and as an advocate for cyberbullying victims. See more at http://tinyurl.com/k7cdybm.

She and her Siberian husky, Phoebe, volunteered at York Hospital in Maine every week to visit patients and also for the Salvation Army's "Tools of Life" program in Portland, Maine, teaching the class how to use the Internet properly and not make mistakes that could stay with them forever.

She lives in New England with her husband, Chris, Buddy the cat, and four fish. In her spare time she likes to garden, walk on the beach, go fishing with her husband, and enjoy a backyard campfire and barbecue (yes, even in the winter). For more information about Hitchcock, visit her personal website at www.jahitchcock.com.